BRITISH COLUMBIA MURDERS

BRITISH COLUMBIA MURDERS

Mysteries, Crimes, and Scandals

CRIME/MYSTERY

by Susan McNicoll

PUBLISHED BY ALTITUDE PUBLISHING CANADA LTD.
1500 Railway Avenue, Canmore, Alberta T1W 1P6
www.altitudepublishing.com
1-800-957-6888

Extreme care has been taken to ensure that all information presented in
this book is accurate and up to date. Neither the author nor the
publisher can be held responsible for any errors.

Publisher	Stephen Hutchings
Associate Publisher	Kara Turner
Editor	Georgina Montgomery
Digital photo coloration	Scott Manktelow

We acknowledge the financial support of the Government
of Canada through the Book Publishing Industry Development
Program (BPIDP) for our publishing activities.

Altitude GreenTree Program 🌲
Altitude Publishing will plant twice as many trees as were used
in the manufacturing of this product.

National Library of Canada Cataloguing in Publication Data

McNicoll, Susan
British Columbia Murders / Susan McNicoll.

(Amazing Stories)
Includes bibliographical references.
ISBN 1-55153-963-2

1. Murder--British Columbia. I. Title. II. Series: Amazing stories
(Canmore, Alta.)
HV6535.C32B75 2003   364.15'23'09711   C2003-911124-5

An application for the trademark for Amazing Stories™
has been made and the registered trademark is pending.

Printed and bound in Canada by Friesens
2 4 6 8 9 7 5 3

Cover: Fan Tan Alley, Victoria, BC
(Reproduced courtesy of the BC Archives)

To Seema Shah, the most awesome
friend and "average reader" anyone could ask for.

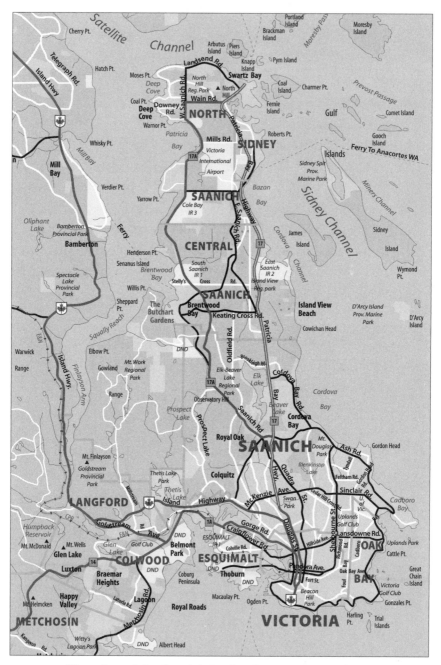

Victoria and the Saanich Peninsula, Vancouver Island,
as it looks today

Contents

Prologue

Wong Foon Sing had been kidnapped and beaten for 14 days by some of the people paid to uphold the law, not break it. After putting a chain around his body and tying it to his feet, they slapped him, punched him and rammed his head into the wall. Blood flowed from his nose and ear. His captives washed the blood off and the next day started the assault again.

The constant buzz inside his head would not go away. They thought he'd been lying and wanted the truth. He told them the same facts he had been stating all along about the murder of nursemaid Janet Smith. The truth made them angry. Now, it appeared, his suffering was going to come to a tragic end.

The men showed him a picture of his wife and told Wong he would never see her again. He was unchained and taken upstairs to an unfinished room with exposed wooden beams. There was a rough scaffold with a chair on it and Wong saw a rope hanging over one of the beams. It had a noose at one end.

"They put me on chair and fix rope on my head,"

Wong later testified. "Man says, 'You tell everything or we kill you. You tell or you be dead.' I say I no can tell anymore. I no know nothing more about poor nursie. Man say again they hang me."

One of his captors pulled the chair out from under him. Wong Foon Sing lost consciousness.

Chapter 1
Arsenic and Cold Shakes

ocal radio personality Rene Castellani undoubtedly thought he was going to get away with it. After all, he had been slowly and methodically poisoning his wife, Esther, for months leading up to that summer of 1965 and no one suspected a thing. Not her family or her doctors, not his co-workers — not even the station receptionist he was planning to marry.

Although Rene had been unhappy in his marriage for a couple of years, the seeds for his scheme were not planted until he began working as a promotions man for Vancouver radio station CKNW in late 1963. His first publicity stunt was a precursor of things to come. He was hired by the station to play the so-called "Maharaja of Alleebara" and pretend he was in British Columbia to announce his plans to "buy" the province. With his exotic outfits and entourage of dancing girls and bodyguards, the phony maharaja was wined and dined by unsuspecting hosts at the Astor Hotel and seen picking up tabs for patrons in bars.

Everyone in Vancouver began talking about the maharaja. Huge signs on the sides of buses proclaimed his desire to buy British Columbia — a prospect that even prompted a few citizens to protest with pickets reading "Keep B.C. British." It was all a scam, of course. It did, however, show Rene's abilities to pull the wool over people's eyes — abilities that would ultimately extend way beyond his job and into his private life. CKNW had found a star in this con artist. He would end up bringing them more publicity than they had ever dreamed of, but not the kind they wanted.

Esther Castellani began to have stomach problems towards the end of November 1964. She tried to live with the condition and even continued working at a children's clothing store. About the same time, she told a friend of hers that all was not well in her 19-year marriage. She had found a letter in her husband's wallet from someone named "Lolly" and suspected he was in a relationship with the woman. When she confronted Rene with her suspicions, he denied anything was going on.

Esther's stomach problems quickly began worsening and she started having abdominal cramping as well. On January 5, 1965, she made the first of nine visits she would end up having with the Castellani family physician, Dr. John Secter.

"She had abdominal pains and nausea," Dr. Secter would later testify. "I examined her and found her to be otherwise normal physically. I told her to watch her diet and gave her medication."

Dr. Secter stated he treated her for gastritis and a possible gall bladder condition. Three times Rene Castellani phoned him in the middle of the night and once in the afternoon to make a house call.

On May 17, 1965, Esther went to Dr. Secter's office and said she felt somewhat better, but four days later her husband summoned the physician to their house yet again. Dr. Secter advised his patient to have a gall bladder X-ray. He would never treat her again.

By now, others in her family were becoming increasingly worried. With this last severe bout of abdominal pain and vomiting, Esther's mother reached the breaking point in her concern for her daughter and she called in a specialist, Dr. Bernard Moscovich. This infuriated Rene who asked his mother-in-law if she did not think he was capable of taking care of his own wife. Regardless of her husband's anger, Dr. Moscovich examined Esther on May 23, 1965, and had her admitted to Vancouver General Hospital the following day.

Meanwhile, back at CKNW, rumours about Rene had been running rampant for some time. He was now billed as The Dizzy Dialer, performing what could best be described as a radio version of the popular old television program "Candid Camera." Rene would phone stores, hotels, and other places and say outrageous things or make ridiculous requests, totally deadpan and convincing. The person on the other end of the line would be taken in and made to look gullible and foolish on the radio. It was a role Rene relished.

His private life, though, was causing concern at the station. Early in 1965, W.J. Hughes, manager of CKNW, had heard talk of a relationship between Rene and the recently widowed station receptionist, Adelaide (Lolly) Miller. Rene was Catholic and married, with a 12-year-old daughter, and Hughes did not want any bad publicity for the station. As he did with his wife, however, Rene denied the relationship existed.

Hughes would later testify that Esther called the station one day looking for her husband. She said he had left for work at 4.00 a.m. that morning explaining he had a very important project, yet when she tried to reach him, he wasn't there. Once again, Hughes spoke to Rene, this time telling him his association with Lolly Miller had to be terminated or the two of them would be dismissed. In May, when it became apparent his words were not being heeded, Hughes called for the pair's firing. Lolly resigned on May 5, but — in a little piece of irony — Rene ended up not being asked to leave at that time because his wife was sick and the station wanted to show compassion. It was then that Esther's condition worsened and she entered hospital. Rene continued working.

As her days in hospital passed, Esther's nausea persisted and she grew weaker. Numbness set in. She gradually lost the use of her arms and legs and was in tremendous pain. She could no longer feed herself or even hold a cigarette. When she went into hospital she was still able to eat, but by mid-June she was being fed intravenously as well. Her white cell count dropped and Dr. Moscovich told Rene that his wife's condition was becoming very serious. They were still searching for a cause and even considered paint poisoning when they discovered Esther had done some painting the previous year at the store where she worked. This theory did not pan out, but Rene would take every new speculation and tell it to anyone who would listen.

It was shortly after the doctors told him his wife

was seriously ill that Rene performed his best-known stunt, one that would play out prominently down the road. In a radio promotion for Bowell McLean Motors (locally known as BowMac), Rene climbed to the top of the BowMac sign on West Broadway at Alder and stayed there for eight days. This was the era of the neon sign rage in Vancouver and BowMac's had been the tallest free-standing sign of its kind in North America when it was built in 1959. (The man who went on to become synonymous with signs in Vancouver, Jimmy Pattison, was BowMac's sales manager. He commissioned Neon Products, which he owned, to build a sign that would outshine that of every other car dealership in town. He succeeded.)

More than one person recommended to Rene just before the BowMac stunt in June 1965 that he not do it because his wife was so sick. But Rene said the radio station owed it to the sponsor — and besides, he added, his wife wasn't really that sick.

"NW's Dizzy Dialer has reached new dizzy heights at the BowMac used car lot," the ads in the papers read. "Marooned high atop a 40-foot tower in a BowMac station wagon, he refuses to come down until BowMac has sold 216 cars." The ads continued to record his achievements, and Rene would also cut into radio broadcasts live throughout the night. After the eight days were up, Rene returned to solid ground.

The doctors treating Esther continued to perform tests as she became sicker day by day. Rene frequently took food in to her (especially her favourite White Spot chocolate milkshakes) to stimulate her appetite. One day in early July, Esther's mother, Mabel Lound, brought in some ground beef and string beans, but it was late in the day and the nurses put the meal in the refrigerator. The next day, Esther's sister-in-law, Sheila Lound, arrived to find Rene trying to feed his wife some of the beef over her protests that she was feeling nauseous.

Mrs. Lound took the dish away and finally, at Rene's persistence, threw the food down the toilet. She would later testify that, outside the hospital room, she asked him what he thought was causing his wife's illness.

"When a house burns down, I don't look for a fire. I look around to build a new one," Rene apparently replied.

A number of people, including the Castellanis' long-time friend Frank Iaci, best man at their wedding, tried to persuade Rene to end the relationship with Lolly Miller, which Rene continued to deny even existed. Iaci told him to stop it and tell Esther there was something to come home to so that she would recuperate faster. As Iaci would state later, Esther had told him that all she wanted to do was get out of hospital and take her daughter with her to live at her mother's.

All this time, the relationship between Rene and Lolly was progressing nicely. Towards the end of June they began telling some of the people in their lives that they were going to be married in a couple of weeks. Rene also told a number of people variously that he had a divorce or one was coming through imminently. On June 29, the pair went to look at a house together that Lolly was interested in buying. They told the builder, Warren Peterson, they were going to be married soon and he asked what name should go on the mortgage. It was decided it should be Lolly's name, but Rene would co-sign to help her get the mortgage. Real estate agent Allan Gillis would later testify in court that the couple came to him in connection with the mortgage. He said they arrived in a CKNW van and told him also of their plans to get married in about two weeks. They agreed to make the application in the name of Mr. and Mrs. Castellani because of their impending marriage and to avoid the expense of a subsequent name change.

Esther continued to deteriorate and became unable even to turn over in bed by herself. A nurse, Lydia Ratzlaff, only saw Rene and Esther together once when she entered the patient's room in answer to a call light.

"She [Esther] wanted the pillows adjusted," Ratzlaff would testify. "It was not a difficult job — it could have been done by anyone."

Arsenic and Cold Shakes

She said that Rene Castellani was sitting in a chair at the foot of his wife's bed. The sick woman, by now immobilized from her illness, was lying on her left side in a position from which she could not see her husband. It seemed she didn't even know he was in the room.

Esther's heart finally gave out on July 11, 1965. She was 40 years old. Rene was reluctant to allow an autopsy on his wife, but finally agreed. It revealed she had died from a viral infection and heart failure.

The day following the funeral, Rene and Lolly Miller had a meeting at the Canadian Imperial Bank of Commerce to arrange a mortgage for the house. However, the bank found Rene had a bad credit rating and advised the real estate agent not to proceed with the sale. Rene explained to the bank that he had been the assistant manager at the Willows Hotel in Campbell River when it burned down in 1963, resulting in a number of deaths. He said he had been greatly affected by the fire and on medical leave for more than a year after it, during which time he fell behind on his payments and developed the poor credit rating.

In truth he had been unemployed for only a short time after the fire, but without checking, the bank agreed there were extenuating circumstances and went ahead with the mortgage. It was under the name of Rene and Adelaide Castellani, because Rene assured the bank that he and Lolly would provide proof of marriage within 14 days.

Two days after Esther's funeral, CKNW generously loaned a vehicle to Rene so that he could take his daughter on a two-week trip to Disneyland. What he didn't tell his employers was that Adelaide Miller and her six-year-old son were going with them.

Back in Vancouver, Dr. Moscovich was dissatisfied with the findings of the autopsy and the apparent cause of death.

"I knew it was heart failure," he stated in court, "but I wanted to know what led up to that."

He went home and studied the history of Esther's case in detail and summarized all the test results from her hospital stay.

"There were many organs involved," he said. "I wanted to know what could have caused the 'gross insult' that caused her death."

After examining the findings, Dr. Moscovich began a process of elimination. He ruled out, one by one, various rare diseases. Eventually, he concluded that some toxic factor was to blame — and the one he came to single out was arsenic.

He arranged to have some of the woman's tissue sent to the city analyst for testing.

Bingo.

Arsenic and Cold Shakes

* * *

Death by arsenic poisoning is particularly horrible and painful.

In its pure state, arsenic is a grey metal. However, it is most commonly found as arsenic trioxide, a white powdery substance that is sometimes used in weed killers and rat poisons. In most murder cases where it's been used, arsenic is stirred into food and ingested by the victim. In Victorian England, this was a popular method for disposing of someone. Though less common a method now, even as recently as April 2003, one person died and many others were seriously sickened when arsenic was added to coffee at a Lutheran church reception in New Sweden, Maine.

A large, one-time amount of arsenic can often be noticed by the victim, so most killers who chose this means resort to chronic poisoning over a long period of time. In small amounts, arsenic is colourless and tasteless.

The symptoms of arsenic poisoning can mimic those of many other illnesses. The most common effect is extreme stomach pain and cramps. Other symptoms include a burning throat and pain, vomiting, and bloody diarrhea. The skin can become cold and clammy and blood pressure can fall dramatically, making the victim dizzy and weak. There can also be spells of paralysis. In time, red blood cells are destroyed and numbness can sweep through the body. Weight loss, visual disturbance, and finally heart failure are often the course of extreme and chronic arsenic poisoning. It is a truly gruesome, and very painful, method of murder.

* * *

The analyst reported his findings to Dr. Moscovich on July 29, 1965, and a couple of days later the police were called in. They went to the Castellani home where, in Rene's presence, they found a can of Triox weed killer under the kitchen sink. They seized it and a number of other household cleaners for analysis.

Dr. Moscovich phoned the coroner and recommended the exhumation of Esther Castellani. This was done, and the results of the second post-mortem sent the investigation into high gear. Things were beginning to unravel for Rene Castellani, albeit somewhat slowly. In October 1965 he was asked to leave radio station CKNW — ostensibly because the quality of his work was deteriorating. (In all the subsequent coverage of the murder, the station would never acknowledge that Rene had been working for them when the murder took place.)

Finally an inquest was called into Esther's death. It

took place over three days in early December 1965. Most of the testimony focussed on the state of the Castellanis' marriage, Rene's extra-curricular activity, the tests done on Esther's body, and the can of weed killer found in their house.

Assistant city analyst Eldon Rideout stated that the tests showed Esther had ingested arsenic regularly over a period of time he set at about six months. He said he'd examined a number of prescriptions and hairsprays given to him by detectives, but found no trace of arsenic in them. However, the can of weed killer contained sodium arsenate, one of the most toxic forms of arsenic. About three ounces was missing from the can. This quantity of the liquid would have contained about 15,000 milligrams of arsenic. A minimum fatal dose contains about 200 milligrams. Rideout estimated the total weight of arsenic found in the body to be about 300 milligrams. He confirmed that three ounces of the weed killer was more than sufficient to have caused Esther's death. There would have been no need for arsenic from any other source.

Dr. Moscovich said that Esther had shown no depressive tendencies and had been very courageous, wanting nothing more than to be able to go home. Her boss at the clothing store described her as an unusually cheerful person.

A number of witnesses also testified they knew about the relationship between Rene and Lolly and their intentions to marry. As well, a nurse from the hospital stated that she saw Rene bring his wife milkshakes on a number of occasions, but she could not recall ever finding any empty milkshake containers in the room.

The three men and three women on the jury deliberated for more than two hours before giving their verdict, which read in part:

"Esther Castellani, 40, of 2509 West Forty-first, who was certified dead at Vancouver General Hospital at 10:45 a.m., July 11, came to her death as a result of arsenic poisoning while a patient in the hospital. We classify the death as unnatural and homicide at the hand of person or persons unknown."

It was another four months — late on April 6, 1966 — before Rene was arrested and the following day charged with capital murder in the death of his wife. Only two days earlier, he and Lolly had applied for a marriage licence. Rene was granted bail of $25,000 and his preliminary hearing, though initially set for May 9, was later postponed until July because of delays in assembling some of the Crown witnesses. Because of this hold-up, Rene's bail was reduced to $15,000. Because he was unable to raise this amount, however, he remained in jail.

Arsenic and Cold Shakes

The preliminary hearing would bring certain facts to light and also lay the groundwork to show the relationship that existed between Rene and Lolly. The city prosecutor, Stewart McMorran, sought to prove that Esther died from arsenic poisoning and that the most likely perpetrator of her murder was her husband.

Several scientific people testified surrounding the findings of arsenic in the victim's body. Poison expert Dr. Harold Taylor, head of pathology at the University of British Columbia in 1965 and executive director of pathology laboratories at Vancouver General Hospital, said that Esther Castellani had been given arsenic for at least five months before her death. He based his time estimate on tests showing high concentrations of arsenic in her hair, nails, heart, and liver.

Dr. Taylor said the arsenic in the heart and liver indicated she must have absorbed the poison one to three weeks before her death or else it was the accumulation from multiple dosages. He concluded that her death from heart failure was a result of chronic arsenic poisoning that affected the heart muscle.

City analyst Eldon Rideout said he conducted hundreds of tests over a three-month period on specimens from Esther's body and found the highest concentration in her hair near the roots, her fingernails near the quick, and the heart and liver. Arsenic is naturally present in the human body in minute quantities — about .03 parts per million for vital organs and one part per million for nails and hair.

When arsenic is ingested it immediately goes to the hair. Since hair grows approximately one centimetre per month, it is possible to shave a victim's hair at the scalp and follow the concentration of arsenic back up the hair shafts to determine when the poison was ingested. In Esther's case, a hair close to the root was found to have 215 parts of arsenic per million — or 70 times the accepted minimum lethal level.

Rideout also said that the three ounces missing from the Triox tin found in the Castellani house was more than enough to account for the arsenic concentrations in her body. However, he couldn't swear the arsenic in Esther's body came from the tin of weed killer.

One damning piece of evidence presented was that Castellani had thrown out an idea for the cause of his wife's illness that had not been given to him by her doctors. He told a business supplier that the weed killer she had been spraying in the garden had poisoned her system and "it was just a matter of time." He did not elaborate and did not mention this suspicion to the doctors who would have tested for arsenic poisoning had they known.

According to Magistrate James Bartman, testimony

at the preliminary hearing ruled out suicide in Esther's death. It also discounted lead poisoning, "leaving only arsenic poisoning." Rene showed no emotion as Bartman committed him for trial on a charge of capital murder.

On October 31, 1966, before an all-male jury, Rene Castellani pleaded not guilty on the opening day of his murder trial. The focus of the proceedings was the progress of Esther Castellani's debilitating illness that, in the latter stages, left her unable to hold anything or feed herself. Evidence would show that she had ingested arsenic during this period which, as Crown prosecutor P.G. Bowen-Colthurst said, left suicide impossible.

The relationship between Rene and Lolly Miller also came front and centre during the trial, especially in light of the fact that by late September 1965 they had begun living together, along with his daughter and her son.

Eldon Rideout again testified as to the high arsenic content he found in Esther's body, and so did Alexander Beeton, also of the city's analyst department.

The pattern of the arsenic "peaks" showing up in the hair followed the periods of Esther's attacks. They also revealed a sharp drop during the time Rene was doing the car promotion at the top of the BowMac sign, although the higher-than-normal arsenic levels in Esther's body still proved she had ingested the poison during this period. At the inquest and preliminary hearing, the defence made note of this to prove Rene could not have done it. At the trial, however, testimony quickly surfaced showing that he not only could, but did, come down from the pole and go to visit his wife in the hospital more than once. After the radio stunt was over, the arsenic readings took a giant leap upwards — and then upwards again at the point she died.

Following Rideout, city pathologist Dr. Thomas Harmon testified that a microscopic examination he conducted on tissues taken from Esther's peripheral nerves showed a shrinking of the nerve fibre and changes in the covering of the nerve. He was convinced that this degeneration was present at the time of death and was consistent with the type caused by chronic arsenic poisoning. Acute poisoning, he said, was a situation in which a person died after a single dose or multiple doses were administered within a short time. In such cases, there was no time for degeneration of the peripheral nerves.

In response to defence attorney Al Mackoff, Dr. Harmon agreed degeneration could have been caused by a lack of vitamins or a diabetic condition, but he also noted that the changes in Esther were much more severe than he had seen in similar cases.

Some of the nurses testified that, besides seeing Rene bringing his wife milkshakes, they had been asked by him to tell Esther's mother to leave the hospital by 8 p.m. so he could visit alone with his wife. Stewardess Audrey Hill, a nurse's aide while Esther was in hospital, also testified that Rene drove her home one night. Hill said that during the ride Rene asked her when she thought his wife was going to die. She had declined to answer.

Three witnesses testified that Rene had denied any relationship with Lolly Miller. The Crown then entered into evidence an application for a marriage licence dated March 31, 1966, and a marriage licence dated April 4, 1966. There was also testimony the two had told others of their marriage plans during the last few weeks of Esther's life. No evidence was produced showing that Rene had been granted a divorce or even that he had applied for one.

The trial lasted nine days, with the Crown calling 46 witnesses. The defence called none and Rene would not testify on his own behalf. On November 10, 1966, the jury took four hours before coming back with a verdict of guilty. Mr. Justice Ruttan then asked the jurors for a recommendation for or against leniency. It only took 10 minutes for them to decide the latter. Rene Castellani was sentenced to hang February 21, 1967.

However, Rene's ability to wiggle out of jams was not yet over. The defence immediately launched an appeal, taking exception to the judge's charge to the jury. While the appeal was considered, Rene was given a stay of execution to March 28, 1967. On March 10, he was granted a new trial by the five appeal court judges. The hanging was off.

With the success of the appeal, a second trial began on September 25, 1967. It would have a few twists the first one did not. For one, in response to the suggestion in the first trial by the defence that Esther had applied the missing ounces of weed killer on her lawn, city analyst Rideout said the weed killer in question (Triox) was not ordinarily used for that purpose because it could kill the grass as well as the weeds.

Also different this time around was that Rene took the stand. Defence attorney Charles Maclean asked him only one question: "Rene Castellani, look at the jury. Did you murder your wife, Esther?"

"I did not," Rene replied.

"Your witness," Maclean then said to Crown prosecutor Martin Toy.

Rene went on to deny he had a temper and contradicted the statements of many witnesses, but he did admit to the relationship between himself and Lolly. He spent three hours on the stand.

A third twist was that Rene allowed his daughter, Jeannine, now 13, to take the witness stand on his behalf. The girl, who had been living with Lolly since her father's arrest, testified that her aunt, Mrs. Gloria Yusep, was "jealous of mom and threatened to kill her."

In the courtroom, Mrs. Yusep cried out the girl's name in horror.

Jeannine went on to state that the day before her mother went into hospital, her Aunt Gloria had been over at their house making jelly for her mother and that her mother got sick right afterwards. She admitted she had never told the detectives about it at the time of her mother's death.

The Crown re-called Mrs. Yusep to the stand and asked about her niece's statement regarding the jelly. She told the court she was not at her sister's house that day, but with her mother attempting to get another doctor for Esther. She also said she did once make the jelly for her sister, but that was at least a month before Esther went into hospital.

In summing up for the jury, defence attorney Maclean said he agreed that Esther Castellani had died of arsenic poisoning and that her husband committed adultery. However, he went on, this did not make Rene a murderer.

"If we're going to hang men for adultery," he declared, "there aren't enough lamp posts in Vancouver to accommodate them."

Crown prosecutor Toy summed up his arguments by saying there were only two questions to answer: How did Mrs. Castellani die? And, who killed her? As the Crown and the defence now both agreed that she died from arsenic poisoning, he continued, that left only "who did it?" to determine. Toy submitted that Rene Castellani had "opportunity after opportunity after opportunity" to slip arsenic to his wife in her food. The motive, according to Toy, was simple. Rene wanted to marry Lolly. Twelve days before Esther's death, Lolly had announced plans to marry Rene and take a trip to Disneyland, so she was expecting marriage. Rene was Catholic and had not discussed divorce with his wife. That left only one way for it to happen.

The jury of nine men and three women was out for more than six hours in this trial, returning several times to seek further instructions from the judge, Justice Victor Dryer. In the end, they again found Rene guilty of murder — and they made no recommendation for mercy.

Before his sentence was announced, Rene looked at the jury and said, "I've been asked three or four times if I killed my wife. I did not kill my wife. May God have mercy on your souls."

And when he sentenced Rene to hang on January 23, 1968, Justice Dryer looked at him and intoned, "...and may God have mercy on *your* soul."

Yet, once again Rene would escape the noose. In January 1968, while he was awaiting the results of an appeal of this second murder conviction, his sentence was commuted following passage of federal legislation restricting capital punishment for five years. In November 1968, however, his appeal was turned down in a unanimous decision of the Supreme Court of Canada.

Rene Castellani stayed in prison until May 1979. When he was freed, he was nervy enough to phone CKNW for a job. Rejected there, he did nevertheless find radio work in two smaller British Columbia communities, first Abbotsford and then Nanaimo. He also got remarried, but not to Lolly Miller who, by that time, had married someone else.

His was a short-lived freedom, however. Rene died of cancer in January 1982.

Chapter 2
Dead Man, Centre Stage

he chicken oath notwithstanding, Wong Gow and Wong On were not believed in 1904 when they declared their innocence in the murder of Chinese theatre manager Man Quong. He had been brutally beaten and then thrown over the balcony onto the stage of his own theatre. It seemed like an open and shut case when two men were arrested for murder after being identified by witnesses as the killers.

In the theatre, though, everything is an illusion — and, as in most good murder mysteries, this one had a twist.

British Columbia's Chinese community was thriving, but it had a dark side. The population of Victoria's Chinatown in 1904 was growing quickly and Chinese immigrants gravitated to a six-block radius in the downtown core. Most of them joined "tongs," essentially Chinese guilds, associations, or secret societies. Tongs were very important to Chinese immigrants because they recreated familiar institutions from home, giving the immigrants a sense of social security in a new land where they were often excluded. Tongs protected their members from outsiders, and fights between warring tongs in China even occasionally found their way to the Chinese communities overseas. Tongs would also play a major role in the murder of Man Quong.

Quong was an actor and manager of the Chinese Theatre, which was located in Theatre Alley off Cormorant Street in Victoria. Both Theatre Alley and the more famous Fan Tan Alley formed the core of Chinese nightlife in the city at the turn of the century. Fan Tan Alley, in fact, had the first gambling houses in British Columbia. Only 60 metres long and too narrow to allow two people to walk through side by side, the alley still held numerous gambling houses and many restaurants to feed the gamblers. Most immigrants were male (often leaving wives and children in China), had low-paying jobs, and lived in rundown rooming houses. They drank

Theatre Alley in Victoria's Chinatown

and gambled to relieve loneliness. Prostitution was rampant and opium houses did a steady business. In fact, opium addiction was becoming a problem in Victoria at that time, although the opium houses were completely legal and the British Columbia government made a great deal of money by imposing annual licensing fees on the operations.

On nearby Cormorant Street, Theatre Alley was also thriving in those days. Slightly wider than Fan Tan Alley, it held the Chinese Theatre which was entered from a wooden staircase in the alley. It was a big room filled with long wooden benches and lit by only a few bare-bulb drop lights. Heat was provided by two wood stoves, and on each side of the stage was a stairway leading to the balcony whose front consisted of a low, white picket fence. Off the balcony, a door led to dressing rooms, including one where Quong lived.

The plays produced were very stylized and similar to today's soap operas. They had innumerable acts that continued for weeks. You could see Act One on Monday and then pick up the story in a later act on Friday. In Chinese tradition, all the cast was male, with female roles being played by men dressed as women. The villain always wore white make-up to be easily recognizable. The orchestra played at intervals throughout the performance and usually consisted of a one-string fiddle, a three-string banjo, drums, and gongs. Scenery was almost non-existent, mainly chairs and wooden planks.

After the performance each night, Quong would make his way to the clubs in Fan Tan Alley where he enjoyed all they had to offer. In early 1904, however, all was not well in Theatre Alley. Quong had been threatened repeatedly for a couple of weeks, although by whom he did not say, and, fearing for his safety, had refused to go out except in broad daylight and in the company of his friends. Since the threats began, he had been unable to do the rounds and he missed all the nightly entertainment. So, on January 31, 1904, Quong decided to bring his friends to the theatre for some revelry instead. He would feel safe there and would have control over who entered.

By midnight the play was over and the actors had left. Shortly after that, Quong's guests arrived. It was close to 12:30 a.m. He vigorously inspected the arrivals for any concealed weapons. He was very tense, but food, Chinese wine, and opium soon lightened the mood considerably for him and the others.

About an hour later, according to eye witnesses, there was a loud knock on the door leading out into Theatre Alley. Quong thought it might be a late guest and opened the door a crack. It was flung back forcefully and two men stood in front of him, with others behind. The intruders rushed at Quong. They grabbed him by his queue (the traditional plaited pigtail the Chinese then wore) to stop his escape and then beat him with iron bars. Carrying his battered body through the door onto the theatre's balcony, they flung it over the edge, more than four metres to the stage below. Quong's body struck a table on stage before landing on the ground.

The assailants quickly disappeared. Some of the guests rushed into Theatre Alley and gave chase while others headed to the police station to report the attack. Constable George Carson was the first policeman on the scene. He found Quong still lying on the stage, in obvious pain but conscious. After helping Quong into a chair, Carson went off to summon Dr. Robinson. When the two returned, they found Quong had been taken to his bed by friends. The doctor quickly realized that Quong was seriously injured and sent him to Jubilee Hospital. He died there about 6 a.m. Some of his friends reported that when Quong realized he was dying, he told them he knew who some of his assailants were and begged that they be arrested. He had given their names to his friends.

Three iron bars reportedly used to beat Quong were found in a small passageway near his room. Later in the morning, Detective George Perdue was added to the investigation. Quong's friends told Perdue that one of the dead man's assailants had been Wong Yuen, a musician at the theatre who had recently seen his salary reduced by the Chinese state. He and Quong had had a previous fight, but things were smoothed out and Yuen was allowed to stay in the orchestra. Nevertheless, witnesses told the court that Quong and Wong Yuen had quarrelled again the night before the assault.

The musician was not to be found after the murder, but two of his cohorts were — Wong On and Wong Gow. They were quickly identified by the witnesses as two of those who had attacked Quong and they were arrested.

The Wongs were infamous in British Columbia as evidenced by this report in the *Vancouver Daily Province* from February 3, 1904:

"[One of the Wongs] in this city has gone to Victoria ostensibly for the purpose of directing the defence of men since arrested. ... Wong Sai Yow, popularly known in the Chinese colony of Vancouver as the Gold Tooth Fellow, went to Victoria on Monday. He bears the reputation of being the leader of the Wong family, which is a very bad lot, and just as many as possible of its members are now being gathered in by the Victoria police. Wong Sai is said to be an ex-convict from the State of Oregon and is said to have been high in the councils of the Highbinders."

On February 8, 1904, the jury at the inquest ruled "murder by person or persons unknown," although that wasn't quite accurate. They did know, because three days later the preliminary hearing of Wong On and Wong Gow for the murder of Man Quong began.

The first full day of the hearing began uneventfully with a drawing of the theatre being shown and Constable Carson testifying where he found Quong's body. Haw Fat Chung, an actor in the Chinese theatre and present at Quong's party, was then called to the stand. This precipitated a major problem over the nature of the oath he would be required to make before his testimony. The oath used in 1904 was a Christian oath, but the Canada Evidence Act allowed substitute oaths for non-Christian witnesses. In the case of Chinese testifying, three separate oaths could be used:

• The Paper Oath — The witness wrote his (or her) name on a piece of paper and, while burning the paper, took an oath that if he did not tell the truth his soul would be consumed by fire just as the paper was.

• The Saucer Oath — On the stand, the witness knelt down, the clerk handed him (or her) a china saucer, and the witness broke it against the box. The witness then took an oath that his soul would be cracked like the saucer if he did not tell the truth.

• The Chicken Oath — A chicken was obtained. The

witness was handed a piece of paper that said words to the effect, "Being a true witness, I shall enjoy happiness and my sons and grandsons will prosper forever. If I give false evidence, I shall die on the street, I shall forever suffer in adversity, and all my offspring will be exterminated. In burning this oath, I humbly submit myself to the will of heaven which has brilliant eyes to see." The witness, court, and jury would then retire to a convenient place outside the building where the oath could be administered. In addition to the poor chicken, a block of wood, an axe or knife, no fewer than three punk sticks (small pieces of rotting wood usually used as kindling), a pair of candles, and Joss paper were also needed. The candles were stuck in the ground and lit. The oath was read aloud by the witness who then wrapped it in the Joss paper. The witness would then place the chicken on the block of wood and chop its head off, set fire to the oath with the candles, and hold the burning paper until it was consumed.

Witnesses in court were usually asked to pick the oath they felt would be most binding on them to tell the truth. With Haw Fat Chung now preparing to take the stand in the Wong trial, the issue of the oath took centre stage. W.J. Taylor, who represented the accused, quoted an authority in which it was asserted the chicken oath was the most binding. The choice was the witness's and

Haw Fat Chung chose the chicken oath. The proceedings quickly came to a halt again because the translation of the oath was so poor that the court interpreter refused to administer it because of "conscientious scruples." An adjournment was ordered until 2 p.m. so that a new form of the oath could be translated into Chinese.

This time, Haw Fat Chung was satisfied and signed the oath. It seemed as though the hearing was at last moving forward — until an argument broke out between the prosecution and the defence over who was responsible for paying for the chicken, punk sticks, and everything else needed for the oath!

The prosecution claimed it was up to the defence to provide the chicken. Taylor refused. George Powell for the prosecution also refused. The judge announced that the case could not go on, but something had to be done to give the prisoners a preliminary hearing. Finally, the prosecution relented and said they would supply the chicken, but they needed time to do so. The judge, wanting to move forward, suggested to the witness that he consider choosing one of the other two oaths. Haw Fat Chung said neither of those would be as binding to him as the chicken oath. An adjournment was called until the next day.

Finally, Haw Fat Chung took the stand. He testified he knew both the accused men and Quong and there had been a fight between Quong and Wong Yuen the night before the murder. At the end of the fight, he said, he had told the crowd to disperse and testified that Wong On told him, "Oh, you're taking Man Quong's part. We'll bring you out and cut you to pieces. ... Look out for tomorrow. You'll die then." Along with a number of others, Haw Fat Chung then fingered Won On and Wong Gow as two of those who attacked Quong with the iron bars before throwing him down onto the stage.

This was enough for the judge, who bound the two prisoners over for trial, to begin May 4, 1904. Most of the evidence at the trial was similar to that presented at the hearing. Dr. Robinson went into more detail regarding the condition of Quong's body after the fall. He confirmed that the cause of death was hemorrhaging and shock. The hemorrhage was from the kidney, which he found to be split in two.

Among those who testified for the defence was Dr. Davie, who stated that no one could be beaten with iron bars without marks showing up on the body. There were none. There were also witnesses for Wong On that proved he was elsewhere that night. On the other hand, eight other witnesses all swore that he and Wong Gow were among the killers.

On May 9, the jury found the two Wongs guilty of murder and Justice Irving sentenced them to be hanged

July 22, 1904. Four accomplices were still at large and the Chinese Benevolent Society issued a proclamation against the Wong clan and offered a reward of $150 for each of the missing four.

By this time, the original detective on the murder scene, George Perdue, had become very suspicious. Nothing added up.

Born in Ontario, Perdue had moved to Vancouver in 1886 (shortly after the great fire that destroyed much of the city). In 1891, at 37 years of age, he joined the Provincial Police. Two years later he became a member of the Victoria City Police, and shortly after that, a detective. Perdue was the first plain-clothes officer on the streets of Victoria. He quickly became well known and respected for his knowledge of those within the criminal element in Victoria and abroad.

While police ineptitude in the early years of British Columbia's history led to many wrong guilty verdicts and unsolved murders, there were also cases where good and thorough police work ultimately saved the day. This would turn out to be one of those times, although luck would also help save the Wongs from the gallows.

In spite of the eye witnesses to Quong's murder, Perdue sensed something was not right about the entire affair. He had listened to the testimony of the doctors who said they could find no evidence on Quong's body that he had been beaten with iron bars. And, while the bars themselves did exist, they showed no signs of having been used to assault anyone. Perdue also had many connections within the Chinese community and rumours started to filter back to him — rumours that the two Wongs were being railroaded to the gallows. Meanwhile, Wong On and Wong Gow had appealed their case on the grounds of an omission on a point of instruction from the trial judge to the jury. Luck was on their side and the Court of Appeals granted them the right to a new trial.

Detective Perdue continued his investigation and some interesting facts started to surface. He had assumed Quong had been feeling threatened because of the fight described by Haw Fat Chung before the night of the murder. Now he was hearing for the first time that Quong had felt threatened for at least a couple of weeks before his death and was expecting some attempt on his life. While the Wong clan did jump in to protect the two accused, Perdue would learn the main dispute in the murder of Quong was between two rival tongs, the See Yups and the Sam Yups. The feud between these two tongs had been going on for many years back in the province of Canton in China and had found its way to the large Chinese communities in both Vancouver and San Francisco. The See Yup men were labourers and the

Sam Yup men were businessmen who controlled the sale of all goods coming from China. The two tongs did interact, but there was always bad blood between them.

Members from both tongs were among the actors used by the Chinese Theatre in Victoria. A See Yup and a Sam Yup had been cast in the same play. One of the scenes called for a fight between the two actors. During the staged fight, one of the men — a Sam Yup member — had gone much too far and seriously injured the See Yup actor. In order that the tong of the injured actor would not lose face, Quong had been requested to pay money to erase the insult. He did not like the idea and had been slow to pay up. After giving him a couple of warnings, the See Yups decided they had to kill him in order to prevent losing further face. As Wong On and Wong Gow were members of the Sam Yups tong, it was simply a bonus to be able to frame them for Quong's murder. In addition to all this information, Perdue discovered that the killers of Quong were, in fact, the very guests who had fingered Wong On and Wong Gow. He would not be able to come up with the actual proof of this, but it was certainly enough information to take to John Langley, the Chief of Police.

Langley, in turn, decided to test the chain of evidence in court. Nearly a year after the murder, eight of the party guests were charged with "conspiring to secure the conviction of Wong On and Wong Gow for the murder of Man Quong on January 31, 1904, by procuring false evidence."

Among those charged was the same Haw Fat Chung whose chicken oath issue had caused such a disruption at Wong Gow and Wong On's preliminary hearing. Apparently, the chicken died for nothing.

The trial of the eight accused men began December 21, 1904. The lawyer for the Crown, Mr. Helmcken, laid out for the jury the history leading up to the case. He told them that the eight prisoners before them had conspired to persuade witnesses to commit perjury and swear that Wong On and Wong Gow had been present when Man Quong was murdered, and that they had taken part in the attack that resulted in Quong's death. Witnesses would now testify, he said, that neither Wong On nor Wong Gow had been present on the occasion. He also hoped to show that the leading men in the fight were Wong Hong and Lum Yuen.

The first witness was Lum Lock who testified that, a few days before the murder trial began in May 1904, Loo Gee Wing had sent for him and asked him to find Lum Sing and Lum Sam. He did that and Loo Gee Wing offered each of them $100 to swear that Wong On and Wong Gow had been present at the fight in the theatre in the early hours of January 31. When they met a couple of days later, he gave the men an advance on the $100 and told them to attend the trial and hear the evidence given by another witness, and then to repeat that story when their turn came to be examined. Lum Lock's testimony was damning.

However, there was no corroborating proof that Lum Sing and Lum Sam had actually received the money, and this presented a problem for Judge Eli Harrison. He felt it was a case of bribery more than one of conspiracy and asked why that charge had not been brought in the first case. In his address he said:

"The Crown must prove its case to my satisfaction, and if I have any doubt I must give the accused the benefit of it. I say, in the first place, I am not in a position to decide on the guilt or innocence of Wong On and Wong Gow … and I find the other accused (the eight men), not guilty. They are discharged."

So, the conspiracy case was thrown out and none of the eight were arrested for the murder of Quong. However, a charge of perjury was made against several of the Chinese who gave false evidence in the Wong On and Wong Gow murder trial. The two innocent victims were still in jail, but their second trial would start in a special Assize court in January 1905 before Justice Archer Martin.

The second trial lasted 14 days, a record for that

time in British Columbia. According to the Crown, there were approximately 15 men in the room during the fight that resulted in Quong's death. However, further evidence actually implicated three of the Crown's witnesses more than the two prisoners. The defence also drew attention to the fact that a number of Crown witnesses in the first trial were not called to testify. This implied they would likely aid the defence.

A most interesting and unusual aspect of this second trial was that Justice Martin called three additional witnesses to the stand himself, without consulting the Crown. All of them had been at Quong's in the early hours of January 31, 1904, and all three testified that Wong On and Wong Gow were not present.

After a short deliberation on February 8, 1905, the jury returned a not guilty verdict and the judge ordered the release of Wong On and Wong Gow. The two had spent more than a year in jail. They had been lucky enough to be granted a retrial on a technicality — but, most of all, they were lucky to have had a suspicious and thorough detective working on the case. Without him, they would have hanged together on the gallows.

Chapter 3
Coward or Victim?

ess than six weeks after James Coward's death, a number of newspapers were reporting that Elizabeth Coward swooned as she was sentenced to hang for the murder of her husband. In a scene never enacted before in the Clinton courthouse, the unconscious woman had to be carried out of the room.

Justice was swift in 1915. Or was it justice?

* * *

Up near Fort St. James in northern British Columbia, the sun had set by 9:30 p.m. on September 6, 1915.

Elizabeth, 32, and her 16-year-old daughter, Rose, were getting ready for bed. Because of the cramped quarters in which the Coward family was living, Elizabeth's husband, James, slept in a makeshift bed in an old sleigh out on the property. The women had just changed into their night gowns when they heard a shot. What happened next is described by Elizabeth in her own words, written in 1916:

"My girl and I held ourselves in locked arms ... [and] for a minute we did not say anything, thinking my husband would come to the cabin, as he knew that we was afraid of being in the woods alone at night, but he did not come. We called to him from the cabin but still no sound. My girl and I was panic-stricken.

"[W]e took a lamp and was going out to the tent. We looked towards the tent, [but] could not see anything. ... My feet would not move, it seemed as if we were nailed to that spot ... [T]here was no man to be had within 3 miles of the place."

At least not one that was alive. James, it turned out, had been shot in the head.

Elizabeth Coward, born Elizabeth Scarper in 1883, was married for the first time at 13 to a man whose last name was Dell. He died a year later, leaving her with a baby. Elizabeth then married a man named Calabrese. Theirs was a tumultuous union and within 10 years divorce proceedings were underway. In the meantime, the couple had six children, three of whom lived. The oldest of these, Rose, would come to play a major part in this story.

There may or may not have been a legal divorce. Elizabeth was very vague about it, but believed she was divorced because she said she'd seen a divorce document. The prosecution would raise the issue of this vagueness at her trial, insinuating that the woman's morals left a lot to be desired. What is clear is that by 1915, Elizabeth was a single mother with four children and she ran a boarding house in California. Things were often hard for the family and at times she had to put her children under the care of the State. There was much evidence in later years, however, that she was a doting mother and very loved by her children.

Enter James Coward. He had found work as a security guard at the 1915 World's Fair, and moved into Elizabeth's boarding house. The two became close very quickly. Whether they married legally or not is unknown, but Elizabeth took the Coward name and the two lived together from then on as man and wife.

What transpired to make them decide to move to the wilds of Canada is also unknown, but on May 19, 1915, James and Elizabeth (without the children) left San Francisco to take up a pre-emption eight kilometres south of Fort St. James, B.C. (A common means of enticing people to British Columbia in the late 1800s, pre-emptions referred to land that could be settled on and eventually purchased from the government.) Perhaps it was the ownership of land that lured them. Or maybe James was running from something. All that is known for sure is that despite selling Elizabeth's boarding house, the Cowards arrived in Canada with almost no money.

Having to build a home to live in on their new land, Elizabeth and James were staying temporarily in a nearby cabin owned by a Mr. Griffith. He was away much of the time.

"Both Mr. Coward and myself worked very hard in trying to build a cabin … to live in," Elizabeth would later write. "We did not have very much money when we arrived here as my husband was told in California he could get all the work he wanted in Canada in the wheat fields, but such was not the case as he could not get a day's work no matter how hard he tried. I did some washing for men in a store in trade for groceries. I was not used to that kind of work but I had to do something to help my husband while he build [sic] our cabin."

Elizabeth missed her children tremendously and she wanted the oldest, unmarried child, Rose, to join them. Rose had been working in a candy store in California, saving up the fare to join her mother in Canada.

Coward or Victim?

Rose's arrival in Vanderhoof in early July did not go smoothly and was, perhaps, a sign of the troubles ahead. Rose's trunk was too big for the wagon James had borrowed and he had to pay someone to haul it to the cabin. The person, a man named Sullivan, gave the job to two Native men from the Carrier Nation, telling them they would get paid on delivery. James refused to pay twice and an argument ensued. This argument would be the basis of the defence at Elizabeth's trial.

The first thing that became abundantly clear with Rose's presence was that the borrowed cabin was barely big enough for two and would certainly not sleep three. James therefore set up a makeshift bed about 90 metres away from the cabin, in an old sleigh that he rigged with mosquito netting and a tent.

The work on a homestead was hard, and nothing in Elizabeth or Rose's life had prepared them for it.

"I was born in New York State and always lived in big cities so living in the country became very hard for me and the work was [too] hard," Elizabeth wrote. "There was not a doctor within 45 miles [70 kilometres] of us and no railroad within the same distance. …

"[W]e did not get fresh meat or milk or vegetables as they had in the store only can goods. We lived on wild berries that grew in the woods. Men who lived there told us that was the trials of homesteading so we tried to get used to it. ...I then took sick because that was the first time in my life I was out in a country or farm."

In spite of their troubles, Elizabeth and Rose became well known in the area and, as would be testified to at the trial, no one ever saw the family fight. They were, said witnesses, very friendly with each other.

On the day James Coward was murdered, he and the two women had worked together on their almost-finished cabin in the morning. In the afternoon, James walked into Fort St. James alone. He returned much later than usual to the Griffith cabin and had a bag of flour for Elizabeth. After eating dinner and setting his place for breakfast he went off to bed.

A few minutes after hearing the shot that night, Elizabeth and Rose showed up at the door of their nearest neighbour, Lucetta McInnes. She had a friend, Florence Whithouse, staying with her and Elizabeth begged the two to come with them to the sleigh.

Florence refused, but Lucetta went. Once back at the cabin, however, the three women lost their courage to go out to the sleigh.

"I remembered my husband telling me that if I was lost in the woods to fire a shot in the air and someone or he would hear the shot. ... [W]e went to the cabin and got a gun we used for rabbits and shot twice. This woman [Lucetta] said we had better go to her house and stay till daybreak."

It was a long night and when Elizabeth went up to the sleigh the next morning — this time accompanied by all three women — she was heard to cry out, "Oh, he is dead!"

Elizabeth Coward's life would never be the same again.

The women returned to the McInnes cabin and decided Rose and Florence would get help from a neighbour, John Roberts. He arrived at 6:30 a.m. and suggested they get another neighbour to stay with them while he went to Fort St. James to report the death.

Constable Rupert Raynor of the British Columbia Provincial Police arrived from Vanderhoof the next morning, September 8. After deciding it was a case of murder, he sent for re-enforcements from Fort (later Prince) George. The same day, the four women packed a few clothes and, with the aid of friends, took the body by wagon to Fort St. James.

In the meantime, Constable Raynor was trying to find the bullet cartridge from a .32 revolver that was found on the ground near the sleigh. On Friday, September 10, "help" arrived in the form of William Dunwoody, who referred to himself as Chief of Police, and D.H. Hoye, Vanderhoof Justice of the Peace. From then on, Elizabeth Coward's fate was sealed.

With some local help, the men searched for two days to find the missing cartridge, completely tearing up the Coward homes and belongings. These efforts yielded nothing until Dunwoody, it seemed, had an idea.

Following closer examination of the bullet that had been removed from James's skull, he redirected the searchers to look for a .38 revolver because he now believed that was the murder weapon, not a .32. Armed with these new instructions, Justice of the Peace Hoye went outside and almost immediately looked under an overturned washtub lying in plain view in the yard — a spot that had evidently not been checked during the previous two-day search. Lying there was a rusted .38 gun.

At this point, Dunwoody decided Elizabeth was guilty and began looking for proof without bothering to go through proper forensic procedures such as fingerprint and ballistics testing (both of which were available at the time). It was never even proven that the bullet from James's skull was fired from the rusted gun. Instead of trying to follow standard investigative methods, Dunwoody decided to set a little test for Elizabeth, one he was sure she would fail. He told her nothing about the .38 gun and returned it to where Hoye had located it.

The day after James was buried, Dunwoody allowed Elizabeth and Rose to go back to the Griffith cabin for clean clothes. Meanwhile, he instructed

Raynor to get to the cabin before the women and hide himself in a spot where he could see the overturned tub. Elizabeth and Rose were joined by Mrs. Murray, at whose home they had been staying in Fort St. James. The women were horrified to see the mess the policemen had made during their search. Finding no clean clothes, they were on the verge of leaving when Elizabeth walked around the side of the cabin and looked at the washtub. Raynor would later testify at her trial that she made a sharp glance at the tub and then paused over it for nearly a minute.

It would be all the proof Dunwoody needed and he arrested both Elizabeth and Rose. Years later Dunwoody embellished this story to say Elizabeth had actually lifted the tub and looked at the gun underneath, but the testimony at her trial never showed that. After she was charged with murder, Elizabeth tried to explain she only looked at the tub while considering if she should wash some clothes. Rose was charged with being an accessory.

Elizabeth was in a daze and hardly able to believe what was happening. She would later write about the day of the arrest and all that followed:

"The officer then got a man to strip us and search us. He placed us in such an embarrassing position that we refused to take off any more clothing and because of that they treated us like dogs. They would not let us go and get our clothes and trunks. To this day [March 1916] we do not know where they are. All our [belongings] that we ever had has been lost. We have nothing."

Elizabeth and Rose were sent south to Kamloops to await their trial. Dunwoody travelled to the United States in search of background information and evidence of a motive. He claimed to have found out a number of unsavoury things about Elizabeth, plus to have learned that she'd taken out a life insurance policy on James before they left California. As none of this supposedly damning information was ever presented at the trial, it's hard to believe any of it was trustworthy.

While in jail, Elizabeth wired her son-in-law in California to say she and Rose were in trouble and needed him to come right away. This he did, but because of standing orders from Dunwoody that no one be allowed to see the prisoners, he was turned away.

From the beginning, Elizabeth believed her husband had committed suicide. On the day the police arrived at the cabin following the murder, she even said that to one of the officers when he purportedly asked her what she thought had happened.

"He hushed me up very quickly," she later wrote, "and told me not to say a word about it to anyone or else we, my girl and I, [would] be sent to prison and be hanged too."

Coward or Victim?

A number of other factors also conspired against her at this point. First, Dr. William Stone, who did the autopsy, had only done one murder prior to this one. James had been shot, according to Stone's testimony, directly up his left nostril and into his brain, splitting it in two. Perhaps a more skilled doctor would have been able to tell if this might have been suicide. Second, Elizabeth was given William Scott as a lawyer and he had never tried a case before. Though the young man was bright and able to unearth some interesting facts during the trial, his inexperience definitely did not help her case. And he was able to see Elizabeth only twice before the murder trial began.

Even if she had had money, which she certainly did not, Elizabeth Coward would still not have had the time between her arrest and the trial to mount anything resembling an adequate defence. Both she and Rose were committed for trial at a preliminary hearing in Vanderhoof on September 18, 1915. Elizabeth's murder trial was to take place on October 6 and 7 in Clinton.

Perhaps because of what the policeman had said to her when she told him she believed James had committed suicide, Elizabeth must have felt compelled to come up with another defence. Why she decided to use her husband's fight with one of the men from the Carrier Nation over Rose's trunk is not known. Her neighbour,

Lucetta McInnes, was very prejudiced and had regaled Elizabeth and Rose on many occasions with scary stories about the local Native peoples. Possibly Elizabeth believed that if Lucetta felt this way, many others would also readily believe one of the men had murdered her husband.

This effort failed miserably, as the man she accused provided an iron-clad alibi. Lucetta and Florence Whithouse also turned on Elizabeth, and their stories of the events the night of the murder strongly differed from the accounts given by Elizabeth and Rose. However, Elizabeth's lawyer, William Scott, was able to show that Lucetta and Florence had talked over their evidence and "smoothed out" any discrepancies. He also raised the question of how, if the police had searched the Coward property so extensively at first, they could have neglected to look under the washtub. Unfortunately, none of Scott's efforts had any impact on the jury.

Very little in the way of evidence really proved Elizabeth guilty. Had Dunwoody carried out the forensic tests he should have, she might well have been ruled out as a suspect. Many of Dunwoody's actions were questionable. A letter from the probation office in Alameda County, California, for example, requested the return of five letters "which were borrowed from this office by

Chief Constable W.R. Dunwoody to be used in the trial of ... Mrs. Coward for the murder of James Coward." The Under Secretary of State in B.C. had to write a response in April 1916 informing the California office that the letters could not be found.

Crown prosecutor N.F. Baird could show no real motive for Elizabeth to kill James. Innuendo and circumstantial evidence was all there was. The most damning piece of evidence had been found not by Dunwoody but by Constable Raynor. He had pulled up the floorboard in the cabin and found a leather-bound notebook belonging to James Coward. The last entry read, in part, "[Rose] threatened to shoot me if I molested the dog in any way."

The court sat for 13 hours on day one of the trial and Judge Denis Murphy sent the jury to deliberate after a long second day, without giving them supper. It took them less than half an hour to find Elizabeth guilty. The following description of the scene is from the *Vancouver Province* October 9, 1915:

"Mrs. Coward is small of stature, of middle age and dark complexion. She is of American parentage and foreign extraction. During the two days of her trial she bore up remarkably well and gave not the least sign of a breakdown but towards the end, especially during the address of the Crown prosecutor, her eyes moistened and she became perceptibly emotional. During the judge's charge she riveted her eyes upon him as though looking for some channel of escape from his carefully weighed words."

She would find none.

A short time after the trial, referring to the gun found under the wash tub, Elizabeth would say, "The gun that my husband was shot with was found under a pail near the cabin we lived in, [but there] is no reason we put it there." A month later, though, she said that Rose, fearing her mother would try to commit suicide as she had tried to do once in the past, had taken the gun and hidden it there. Either way, if Elizabeth or Rose had committed the murder, it is highly unlikely they would have left the gun around to be found. They had had plenty of opportunity to dispose of it.

Elizabeth also continued to believe that James had been distraught enough to have taken his own life.

"He and I talked about the long winter ahead of us and no money," she later wrote. "...[H]e was very disappointed although he tried the very best for us. So he was worrying very much and so was I. No one knew of our financial circumstances, but ourself [sic]. I was worrying myself sick because my husband was not like he was in San Francisco, California, always cheerful. ...I am satisfied my husband met death by his own hands, as one knows their own troubles first."

One of the strongest arguments against Elizabeth Coward having killed her husband was where that murder would have left her and Rose. "There my girl and I was alone in the woods — no money, no house, no friends and stranded," she would write. Elizabeth would have needed a very good reason to put herself and Rose in that position.

However, all that was clear on October 7 was that the jury had found her guilty.

If Elizabeth had been surprised at her arrest and shocked at the guilty verdict, then it wasn't surprising she fainted when Justice Murphy sentenced her to hang in Kamloops on December 23, 1915. This gave her the singular distinction of being the first woman in British Columbia to be sentenced to death.

Her only consolation was that all charges against Rose were dropped.

Whether the furore that followed developed because people truly believed Elizabeth Coward innocent, or because a woman had been sentenced to death, cannot be known. Almost immediately, petitions for clemency arrived in droves, one containing 30,000 signatures. The fact that the conviction was obtained almost exclusively on circumstantial evidence obviously played a role as well. On December 12, 1915, the federal Cabinet decided against the hanging, and within days the Governor-General had signed the commutation to life in prison. If the authorities thought this would be the end of the case, they were sadly mistaken.

Elizabeth was sent to Kingston Penitentiary in Ontario to serve out her sentence and Rose returned to San Francisco where she soon married. But the fight to get Elizabeth out of prison was only just beginning. Vancouver lawyer J. Edward Bird joined the defence team and in short order produced an affidavit from Rose declaring that James Coward had propositioned her.

In the early years following Elizabeth's conviction, the many letters and petitions written by her and by others on her behalf to the Minister of Justice pointed to her innocence as the reason she should be released. Slowly the tone of these changed as new information came to light, indicating that there were mitigating circumstances if she was, indeed, guilty. Through all the speculation Elizabeth maintained her innocence.

In 1915, Rose had sworn that her mother was with her when James Coward died. In a letter to the Minister of Justice in May 1918, however, Rose wrote, "Now we all know my mother was guilty. I think my poor mother had her cause. Of course it may not seem that way to you."

Whether she believed this new version of events or

not, Rose may have felt she had a better chance of obtaining her mother's release if she admitted her mother had done it. In Bird's affidavit and these excerpts from the 1918 letter, Rose showed a different side to life with James Coward.

"Before Mr. Coward's death, he had [threatened] to leave my mother when she was in the family way," she wrote. "After he heard [about] it he said, 'How do I know that it is mine.' That was an awful thing to say to her. Of course, mama took something to stop [the pregnancy]. He certainly was an awful disagreeable person. ... He was very insulting to me when I was there."

She continued, "He was always after me to go with him in the wagon where he slept. I was then only 16. And when he found out that I would not go with him he called me every name he could think of. I was not working or giving any money for my board and he said I should pay for it in some way.

"All put together," the letter goes on, "don't you think it was enough to set a person crazy. To tell the truth I really think my mother was out of her mind. ...I guess you think it was funny I did not tell of myself on the trial. Well, I was backward, [and] it seemed awful to say anything like that in front of a lot of people. I did not realize what it meant then but I do now."

J. Edward Bird alluded to the "just cause" factor for

Elizabeth Coward in a letter he sent to the Minister of Justice in 1917:

"As I have acted for this woman now for some time," he wrote, "I unhesitatingly say that I am of the opinion that she is a woman much sinned against. ... [James Coward's] conduct towards this woman was almost unthinkably cruel...and then [he] so conducted himself towards the oldest daughter as to make the life of both one of constant dread."

Bird concluded, "I feel that she was driven desperate, and had she told the real truth, instead of trying in her desperation to manufacture a story for her safety, there would have been real hope of her being acquitted."

In 1918, the U.S. Commissioner of Immigration agreed that Elizabeth Coward was an American citizen and that if she were released she would be permitted to return to the U.S. The Superintendent of Immigration in Ottawa then ordered her deported on her eventual release from prison.

By 1920, the basis of all the requests had changed, now focusing on Elizabeth's ill health and her family's desire for her return. According to Elizabeth and the family, she was on death's door for three years, but every time the doctor made a report, it was not strong enough to obtain her release. She was definitely going for the pity factor at this point, but it was true she was physically wasting away and had trouble walking. Her eyesight was also deteriorating, and doctors often had to give her morphine for the pain in her stomach.

In 1921, word reached Rose that it was being said she had testified against her mother at the original trial and that was one of the reasons Elizabeth was not being released. Rose moved quickly to dispel this belief, stating in a letter that "there sure must be a big mistake as there isn't anything in this world that would make all of the family happier than to have our own dear mother home. ...My mother is the best mother that ever lived. She sure was a good mother to us and we were always happy with her."

The letter had some effect. Moreover, by 1921 it began to look like all the talk of Elizabeth being seriously ill was coming true. Still, not until after the review of a March 22, 1922, report from the surgeon at Kingston Penitentiary was Elizabeth finally given her release. By then, neuritis in her leg had made her bedridden, her eyesight had worsened considerably, and the constant attacks of gastritis were causing her to steadily lose weight. The final blow — which tipped the scales in her favour for release — was that a benign growth had appeared in her left thyroid gland and was enlarging. The surgeon said an operation would be required in the near future to remove it.

On March 23, 1922, the Chief of the Remissions Branch, Mr. Clarke, acknowledged that further confinement would likely prove fatal and he authorized Elizabeth's release. The 39-year-old woman was handed over to the immigration department and deported on March 29, 1922, not quite seven years after the death of James Coward.

The Minister of Justice would receive one more communication regarding Elizabeth Coward — a letter from Rose thanking him for his kindness in releasing her mother back to her.

Chapter 4
Justice Denied

ore than 30 wounds had been dug into her body with a knife on that snowy evening in 1943. Finally, her jugular vein was cut and she stopped fighting her attacker. But those physical violations were not the only ones 15-year-old Molly Justice would suffer. For more than 50 years, the police would be virtually certain who her murderer was, but would never charge him. Why?

The death of Molly Justice would become a murder mystery in three acts spanning half a century. Act I began in 1943.

Act I

Anita Margaret "Molly" Justice was a "mature for her age" young woman who worked as a seamstress at a Victoria garment factory. She was well liked and had lots of friends. On January 18, 1943, she headed home right after work, out to Saanich, a municipality north of Victoria. She carried her purse and two packages as she boarded the Vancouver Island Coach Lines bus at Carey Road and University Street. Most of the regulars on the bus route knew her, and Gerald Dunn later testified he had been sitting next to her that evening as the bus pulled out at 5:50 p.m.

The dark winter evening was made even darker by a war-time ban on lights. However, the area near the railway tracks beside Swan Lake — the area where Molly's attacker lay in wait — had no lights anyway. She did not like walking the shortcut along the tracks, but because it was much faster than the street route, she usually took it. She stepped off the bus on Seymour Street near the Saanich Fire Hall at 6:10 p.m. The bus driver remembered seeing her walk away. She was wearing a black skirt, brown sweater, and green-grey plaid coat. Snow was beginning to fall, but the galoshes she wore kept her feet dry. Other than the killer, the driver was likely the last person to see Molly alive.

Back at home, Molly's family was not concerned

when she did not arrive for dinner. She lived with her brother, Robin, and widowed mother, Muriel Justice. Also living with them was Muriel's future husband, D'Arcy Martin, and his son, Patrick. The four of them assumed Molly was eating in town.

Swan Lake was a popular location that winter, with temperatures having been cold enough to freeze the water's surface. Skaters were out in force. Saanich fireman Arthur Logie and his wife had been watching the skaters after dinner and at 9 p.m. decided to head home along the tracks. Near where Darwin Road intersected the railway tracks, Arthur's foot struck something. He picked up one small package and then another. The couple decided to take them home to see if there was a clue as to who owned them.

Under a light back at the house, Mrs. Logie gasped when she looked at the packages. Her husband just stared at them. Both parcels were covered in blood.

It was 9:30 p.m. when Sergeant Eric Elwell of the Saanich Police received Arthur Logie's call about his disturbing discovery. He and Constable Victor Smith raced to meet Logie at the spot where he had found the packages. Seven to 10 centimetres of snow had fallen that evening, which did not help the men as they began searching the area with flashlights. Half an hour later, however, Constable Smith called out to the other two that he'd found something. About 27 metres from the tracks, Molly Justice lay face down, arms stretched out above her head. The coat and skirt she wore were pulled up over her head and arms.

With the snow covering everything, there was little the police could do that night. Sgt. Elwell stationed an officer to guard the murder scene and drove the body of Molly Justice to the morgue. The family was called and D'Arcy Martin went to identify the body.

The snow again hampered police efforts the next day to search for clues in the area of the killing. Sgt. Elwell found numerous spots of blood in the 36 metres between where the parcels and the body were found. There were signs of a scuffle in three places along the tracks. The young woman had obviously struggled valiantly to save herself, but no one in the area reported hearing any screams. Hair was found under her nails, but no skin. And no hospital reported anyone showing up with a scratched face.

Word spread quickly through Saanich about Molly's death and concerned citizens began angrily blaming the dim-out regulations in place at the time. The rule of no lights after dusk had been instituted at the request of American military authorities. On January 21, to allay fears voiced by parents and students, the Saanich School Board announced that the two high schools in the region would open later in the morning. This would allow students to leave for school in daylight.

The same day, Vancouver criminologist Inspector J. Vance arrived to help Saanich Police with their investigation. Fingerprint expert David Donaldson had also been brought in to help.

A $250 reward was posted by Saanich Municipality and it was matched by D'Arcy Martin. Although Molly's purse was missing, Chief of the Saanich Police, Josiah Bull, ruled out robbery as the motive because of the severity of the attack. On January 25, Sgt. Elwell obtained and executed a search warrant on the Justice home at 861 Brett Street in Saanich. The police had heard rumours that Molly had been killed at home and then dumped where she was found. The rumours were quickly put to rest when hair samples seized from the Justice house were compared with those found under Molly's nails. There was no match, and police excluded all occupants of Molly's house from further suspicion.

Under Dr. E. Hart, the coroner's inquest took place on January 29, 1943. It began on an interesting note. Police had presented three women to be part of the jury. Dr. Hart said they couldn't serve because the Coroner's Act called for "male British citizens" to sit on the jury. Substitute jurors had to be chosen from among the spectators.

The post-mortem had been done by Dr. J. Moore, and he described in detail the results of the horrific attack on Molly's body. He found a six-centimetre cut on the inner part of the left thigh, multiple bruises on both knees, abrasions on the right knee and right thigh, and nine wounds on the right side of the neck. There was also a wound under Molly's chin, bruises and abrasions on the face, two scalp wounds, a cut on the back of the left hand, four wounds on the right hand, a wound on her forehead, and bruises, abrasions, and three wounds on her back. Her right jugular vein had been cut and her left lung punctured. Dr. Moore also stated that he'd found a brain hemorrhage. He said Molly had not been raped.

"The cause of death was hemorrhage," Dr. Moore would later testify. The police believed that most of the damage had been inflicted by a small knife.

The contents of the two packages were also revealed. One was a second-hand pair of shoes and the other was a sweater Molly had bought as a gift for her brother. The jury returned with the obvious verdict of murder by "person or persons unknown."

By February 4, the snow had begun to melt rapidly and a more thorough search of the murder area was possible. Near the edge of Swan Lake, Sgt. Elwell turned over an inverted bucket and found Molly's purse and a cigarette lighter bearing the initials "R.L." There was no blood on the purse and the only fingerprints on the lighter were Molly's.

Molly Justice was buried on February 9 and the hunt for her killer seemed to stall. Then, three months later, on May 16, an event happened that changed the course of the investigation.

An 11-year-old girl named Joan was outside playing with her two younger brothers. They ran off and she chased after them. A youth approached the three children and persuaded them to go onto the lake with him in a rowboat. He finally took them back to shore and said whichever one of them drew the longest straw had to stay with him. He made sure it was Joan. Her brothers ran away and the youth dragged Joan into the bushes, where he exposed himself and attempted to rape her. He threatened her with a pocket knife and said he'd slit her throat and murder her "the same as Molly Justice was murdered." He also said he'd kill her if she told anyone about him. Fortunately, Joan managed to escape and ran to a nearby house.

Joan's parents took the traumatized girl to the police. They questioned her and later showed her a photograph of a person whom she immediately identified as her assailant. She then went home — and never heard from the police again. For 50 years, she believed the guilty man went unpunished, a thought that only added to the pain she always carried around with her.

In fact, the person in the photograph had been charged. On the same day Joan was attacked, 15-year-old Frank Hulbert (born Frank Pepler) was arrested by Constable Smith of the Saanich Police. The young man was also questioned about the Molly Justice murder. Although he claimed not to know Molly, in later testimony he said he had bought some clothes at the factory where she worked and had seen her there. Hulbert pointed the finger instead at William Mitchell, a co-worker of his at a paint plant. According to Hulbert, Mitchell had admitted to him on January 19 he was the killer. The police took Hulbert to the scene of the murder, where he passed on a number of details he said Mitchell had given him, including the locations where the parcels, Molly's body, and her purse and lighter were found.

Hulbert was convicted of the indecent assault of Joan and sentenced on June 3, 1943, to an indefinite term at the Boy's Industrial School in Coquitlam. Two days later, a search warrant was executed on William Mitchell's belongings at a logger's camp and, on June 12, Hulbert gave a written statement alleging that he himself had been indecently assaulted by Mitchell. On that charge, Mitchell was arrested. Sgt. Elwell also obtained a search warrant for Mitchell's room in Victoria and discovered a small knife that appeared to have traces of human blood on it. William Mitchell, 49 years old and a man with no criminal record, was charged with the murder of Molly Justice on June 17, 1943. The other charge of indecent assault on Hulbert was subsequently withdrawn.

Mitchell's preliminary hearing opened July 2, 1943. Much of what had been brought out at the inquest was part of the hearing. The only new evidence came from Hulbert, who said Mitchell confessed to him the day after the murder. Hulbert was caught up a couple of times by defence attorney Patrick Sinnott. According to Hulbert, the defendant told him he had murdered the girl with a rock and a pocket knife and then went home to wash the knife in the bathroom. Alfred Phelps, at whose house Mitchell was boarding at the time of the murder, testified there was no running water at the house on January 18 because of frozen pipes. Hulbert also said Mitchell left work early that day (work ended at 5 p.m.) so he could lie in wait for Molly Justice. However, Lewis Kamann, a co-worker of the two men, said he had seen the accused at 5:15 p.m. at the paint plant. And when Mitchell stated he had cut his finger with the pocket knife police found, a first-aid man from the plant verified this fact.

In the end, the only evidence the Crown had was the testimony of the youth, Frank Hulbert, who had previously been convicted of the assault on Joan.

William Mitchell spoke out in his own defence on July 8, 1943.

"Your honour," he said, "I had nothing to do with murder. I know nothing about it. I did not know such a girl existed. ... I was never in the vicinity of Saanich."

Nevertheless, Magistrate Henry Hall committed Mitchell for trial. Hulbert was returned to prison and then to the Boy's Industrial School.

Frank Hulbert, who would play a key role in all three acts of this murder, was born Francis James Pepler on June 13, 1927, to Thomas Pepler and Mary Jane Pepler. He had stated his father died when he was three. His mother later remarried and the boy would go by his stepfather's name of Hulbert — except when it served his purpose to use Pepler.

By coincidence, British Columbia's Deputy Attorney General in 1943 was a man named Eric Pepler. It was a possible familial connection between Frank Hulbert and Eric Pepler that would muddy the waters of a murder that was already murky enough. Eric was the son of a Francis Edward Pepler and had been born in 1890 in Barrie, an hour north of Toronto. On more than one occasion, Hulbert would refer to Eric Pepler as his uncle, although there was never any proof that the two were related. Checking by later researchers showed that Hulbert's father, Thomas Pepler, had been born in Toronto in approximately 1889 to a father whose name did not appear on his birth certificate. However, no clear relationship between him and Francis Edward Pepler has ever been established.

In the months preceding the trial of William Mitchell, E. Warren of the Saanich Police Commission wrote to Attorney General R. Maitland asking to have the trial moved to the spring of 1944. He received a reply informing him that the Mitchell prosecution was in the hands of Eric Pepler. Meanwhile, Eric Pepler wrote to Maitland, stating, "[I] do not now want to take this case for various reasons and feel strongly that other counsel be appointed." The prosecution of the case was handed over to lawyer Gordon Cameron. Warren's request to move the trial date was denied.

The murder trial of William Mitchell began on November 1, 1943. The main focus of the prosecution was Hulbert's testimony. This time, in response to Hulbert's remark that Mitchell left his job early on the day of the murder, work sheets were produced by the defence proving he did not. As well, Hulbert acknowledged under cross examination that he had been guilty of indecent offences on five occasions. When asked, he also admitted that his last name was legally Pepler.

It quickly became evident that the crowd in the courtroom did not believe Hulbert. When the jury acquitted Mitchell after three days of testimony, the courtroom erupted into cheers and loud applause.

On November 14, Hulbert was escorted back to prison by Constables A. Quinn and Jack Lockie of the B.C. Provincial Police. During this trip he stated that he hated Mitchell and "would do the same to him as he did to Molly." Hulbert made a number of comments that indicated he had been at the murder scene, but told the officers if they tried to use his comments against him he would deny making them. He also told them Eric Pepler was his uncle. In their reports about the conversation, both constables recounted what Hulbert had said. In his report, Constable Quinn wrote that when he reported the statements to Sgt. Elwell, Elwell said Hulbert had told him the same story. Elwell then asked Quinn, "What can we do about it?" He also added that Hulbert said he was in a "passionate fog" at the time he was in the vicinity of Molly's murder.

Based on that information, Warren arranged to have a psychiatric assessment done of Hulbert to determine if the "fog" was as a result of an injury Hulbert may have suffered in an accident. He wrote to Eric Pepler to inform him of this fact. Pepler assured him of the

Provincial Police's support of the Saanich Police. At this point, Warren requested copies of the two police reports regarding Hulbert's confessions. Pepler agreed, but pointed out they were confidential reports for police purposes only.

Dr. George Davidson carried out Hulbert's assessment on December 4, 1943. He concluded, "I believe this boy is probably of dull normal intelligence. ... I felt satisfied at the time of doing the examination that he was telling the story as he thought it would best suit his case. ... [I am] almost certain that he was deliberately being untruthful."

In January 1944, William Mitchell was awarded libel damages of $1,000 against the *Victoria Daily Times*. That same month, Hulbert was convicted of three counts of buggery and sentenced to three concurrent one-year sentences. In June 1945, he was released into his mother's custody, but 11 months later was convicted in another case of contributing to juvenile delinquency and again sentenced to a year in jail.

A postscript to Act I took place in 1948. By this time, Lewis Kamann, former co-worker of both Hulbert and Mitchell, was a Victoria police officer. He had never believed Hulbert's story and felt the young man knew facts only the killer would know. He was in the police station once when Hulbert was brought in overnight.

On seeing Hulbert, Kamann said, "So, they finally nailed you for the murder of Molly Justice?"

Hulbert replied, "Sure, I killed her — you prove it."

Kamann passed the news on to the desk sergeant, but he heard nothing more.

Act II

Act II opened in 1967 with an anonymous letter to the Vancouver City Police. Although it contained many inaccuracies, it triggered another investigation into Molly Justice's murder.

The interest in her murder had actually been brewing again for a few years. In 1956, Saanich Police Chief Josiah Bull encouraged Detective Sergeant Robin Stewart to take the Justice file and work on it. In spite of Eric Pepler having given the Saanich Police permission to obtain copies of the November 1943 reports of Constables Quinn and Lockie about Frank Hulbert's statements, these and other documents were missing from the Saanich file. Det. Sgt. Stewart only found out about them when he obtained access to the Attorney General's files in the 1960s. Former Attorney General Pepler had died in 1957.

On October 25, 1967, five officers from the RCMP and the Saanich Police visited Hulbert in Port Alberni, the town where he was then living, about two hours' drive northwest of Victoria. At the police station in Port Alberni, he confessed that the evidence he'd given in the William Mitchell murder trial in 1943 was false. He said he had lied because he didn't like Mitchell. He did not explain how he knew details of the murder and at no time did he admit his own guilt in it. According to all reports, at no time in the investigation were the hair samples taken from under Molly's nails used to rule out either Hulbert or William Mitchell in her murder. Why this did not happen is unknown.

On October 27, Hulbert was arrested and charged with public mischief for having lied to police 24 years earlier. He was taken the next day to police cells in Saanich.

Two key events happened at the jail. The first was that Victoria lawyer Louis Lindholm arrived at the police station when Frank Hulbert was being processed. He spoke through a door to Hulbert and told him he did not have to talk to police without a lawyer. One of the officers, Det. Sgt. Stewart, said Lindholm arrived 20 minutes after they did and said he'd been instructed by the Attorney General's office to go to the police station and "look after Mr. Pepler's rights." The Attorney General's office has always denied they sent Lindholm.

The second event occurred a little later. An undercover officer placed in a cell with Hulbert said the suspect confessed his perjury in the Molly Justice murder trial of William Mitchell. He also told the undercover officer that perhaps he *had* killed Molly Justice and that was why he knew so much about the murder, but he just didn't remember. Although he didn't recall killing Molly, he was said to have uttered, "Something tells me I must have."

On November 13, an order was made to transfer Frank Hulbert to adult court (since he was now 40 years old), where he was charged with perjury. At his first trial in February 1968, he was convicted of the offence, but in July the conviction was squashed on appeal and a new trial ordered.

Det. Sgt. Stewart had been convinced of Frank Hulbert's guilt all along. On a number of occasions he had asked the senior prosecutor at the time, J. Anderson, to file murder charges against Hulbert, but was turned down. Now he asked again, fearing Hulbert was going to beat the perjury charge. He laid out an entire list of who would testify and what they would say. This time, Anderson also asked for advice from the Ministry of the Attorney General. Neil McDiarmid, Director of Criminal Law with the ministry, wrote to Anderson on August 6, 1967, advising against charging Hulbert with murder.

In January 1969, Frank Hulbert was again convicted of perjury and sentenced to five years in prison.

Act III

Frank Hulbert died in February 1996. A couple of weeks later — and unrelated to his death — the *Victoria Times-Colonist* printed an article on unsolved murders in British Columbia. There was no mention of Molly Justice in it. Molly's sister-in-law, Marjorie Justice, saw the article and phoned Inspector Al Hickman of the Saanich Police. In June 1996, after examining the case one more time, Hickman publicly named Frank Hulbert the killer of Molly Justice and said the police had closed the file on the murder.

"I don't think there can be any doubt that Hulbert did it and he would have been convicted of second-degree murder," Inspector Hickman stated at the time.

That was the end of the murder story, but not the end of the controversy. Hickman talked about a probable connection between Frank Pepler Hulbert and Eric Pepler and said he felt this was why the investigation had stonewalled. He also pointed to the number of different confessions Hulbert had made to various people. The word "cover-up" was liberally thrown around. Hickman's comments prompted a public debate about why Hulbert was never charged. Was it because he was underage? Or because he might have been related to

Eric Pepler? Or because the authorities believed they didn't have enough solid evidence to convict him?

All these possibilities were given a great deal of press in 1996. The hint of impropriety prompted then Attorney General Ujjal Dosanjh to launch an investigation into the conduct of the authorities involved in the case. Dosanjh appointed Martin Taylor, a former judge of the B.C. Court of Appeal, to investigate. Taylor did so, preparing a thorough and lengthy report on the Molly Justice murder and the events during the years that followed it. He stated he found no evidence of a cover-up and that he was not able to prove, or completely disprove, any blood relation between Frank Pepler Hulbert and Eric Pepler.

"It is impossible to say today that Frank Hulbert ought to have been charged with the murder," Taylor surmised in his report. "There are grounds on which a police officer might ... have believed him guilty of the crime."

In the end, Frank Hulbert never had to pay the price for his deed, but finally being named the killer provided Molly and her family some long-denied closure.

Chapter 5
DNA: Dog Nails Assailant

e was a poor elderly man with few possessions, but Vernon resident Daniel Schraeder had friends who cared about him. And his dog would not only give up his life to try and protect him from death, but would ultimately help to nail his master's killer — albeit six years down the road and miles away in California.

The Schraeder murder would also become one of the first cases for British Columbia's provincial Unsolved Homicide Unit, formed in 1996.

* * *

The call came in shortly after 7 p.m. on January 18, 1991. "There's been a fire in Dan Schraeder's house," the male voice said.

By the time the fire truck reached Schraeder's white bungalow at 4106 26th Street, the fire had long since extinguished itself. The firemen found the origin of the fire in the basement. They immediately suspected it was arson and that the fire had been started to cover up something else. They were right. What they found on the main floor was far more than lingering smoke and soot.

Lying across the bed was the bludgeoned body of 81-year-old Daniel Schraeder, his empty wheelchair close by. While the fire had considerably damaged the basement and caused smoke damage in other parts of the house, there had also been an unexpected piece of luck. What the killer had not counted on was the heat from the flames causing a copper water line overhead to separate. The water sprayed out and doused the fire. The death scene was nicely preserved for the members of the RCMP.

Dan Schraeder's body was covered with a sleeping bag and there were obvious injuries to his head. The autopsy concluded that the blow that killed him was likely the one to the left temple area of his skull. Nearby was what appeared to be the murder weapon — a blood-splattered hammer.

Police also found fire soot under the sleeping bag which made them think initially that Schraeder might have been moved after he was killed. They would later determine, however, that the smoke from the fire had caused the sleeping bag to rise up slightly, allowing soot to drift beneath.

And one more grisly discovery was made on the property. In a shed at the back, police found a green garbage bag containing Schraeder's mutt, Chico, also with a crushed skull. There was a great deal of blood on both bodies.

Except for Chico, Dan Schraeder had lived alone in the house for 20 years. A pensioner without much money, he spent most of the time in his wheelchair. Friends checked in on him regularly, and it was one of those friends who called in the fire. Overall, however, Dan's was a lonely existence, and one that would make him easy prey for Billy Faulconer.

The Vernon RCMP quickly had William (Billy) Faulconer in their sights as a suspect. When they had surveyed the murder scene, they'd found a distinctive red-and-white baseball cap. One of the officers recognized it as belonging to Billy.

A heavy drinker, Billy was known to have a vicious temper. The 33-year-old also had a long record of arrests for picking fights, being drunk, attacking senior citizens in the park for money, and mistreating animals. But was he capable of murder?

Coincidentally, Billy had been arrested on a drunk and disorderly charge the same evening of the Schraeder murder and was already in jail. The officers tracking his movements earlier that day found out he'd been at his mother's house. Pat Faulconer told them her son had changed his clothes, leaving behind a pair of jeans in the garbage. The officers retrieved the jeans and discovered blood on them.

The case against Billy was gaining momentum. A friend of Dan's told police that Billy had shown up at the elderly man's house the night before the murder, but she refused to allow him in. Afterwards, Dan had told her he was afraid and that Billy had threatened to kill him.

In 1991, DNA testing was not yet widespread and not available in Canada. Nevertheless, the officers had the foresight not only to take a sample of Dan's blood, but of Chico's as well. Serology tests were done on the blood found on the jeans in order to determine blood type. The results of a sample of the blood only showed it was the same type as both the victim's and the suspect's, but could not be narrowed down more than that.

The next step in the investigation was to establish the time of death. The best the pathologist could determine was that Dan died sometime between noon and

2 p.m. on January 18. Since Billy had a solid alibi for those two hours — he had been at his mother's house — there was not enough evidence to move forward. The RCMP were convinced he was guilty but, based on the existing evidence, they couldn't yet charge him with the brutal murder of a defenceless old man and his dog.

In 1997, however, a turn of events would jump-start the investigation again and give detectives many new tools for re-examining the case.

British Columbia's Unsolved Homicide Unit was formed towards the end of 1996. It has the distinction of being the first such unit (or "cold case squad") created in Canada, as well as one of the largest now in existence in North America. Made up of 16 RCMP officers and four members of the Vancouver Police Department, the unit began looking at hundreds of "unresolved" suspicious deaths — unresolved as opposed to unsolved, Sergeant Trent Rolph likes to point out.

A sergeant in the Drug Enforcement Branch of the RCMP, Rolph was transferred as a constable to the newly formed unit in 1996 and was with it until April 2003.

"Whenever I'm asked if we have solved another case," Sgt. Rolph explains, "I say 'We always solve them. *Proving* it: that's another story.'"

The killer is often identified in the initial investigation of a murder, he explains, and then, for a variety of reasons, the police cannot nail down the case enough to go to trial. So, what are the criteria for choosing a murder for consideration by the unit?

For one, there has to be a solid foundation, Rolph says. "It has to have been investigated well in the first circumstance."

For another, it has to have a pretty definite suspect. "If the case was clearly a 'who dunnit,' then it had its best chance of being solved at the time," Rolph notes. "We obviously cannot go back now and do neighbourhood enquiries, so all that information is gone."

If there is a solid suspect, the police look at where that person is and whether he (or she) is likely to re-offend. If he is, they move him to the top of the list. However, if he's in custody and declared a Dangerous Offender, they know his chance to re-offend is nil.

Two other important factors in choosing cases are the presence of DNA material and whether or not there is "hold-back" information. Hold-back details could be the type of weapon used, exactly how the victim was killed, or how the victim was tied up, says Rolph.

"There are certain pieces of information, hold-back information, that should never get out. The press, especially in the States, really pressures investigators to give up information they have no business giving up."

Cost is also always a factor in choosing which murders to pursue. "There have been cases where we know who the killer is, but it will take half our yearly budget to prove it," Rolph explains.

In the Schraeder case, the cost was a positive factor, as the investigation was expected to be relatively inexpensive to pursue.

Once they have decided to investigate an old murder, the unit officers assigned to it sit down and read everything in the file. This can take a week or a month depending on the complexities of the case. They talk to any available officers who were involved originally. Unless it suits their purposes, they rarely let it be known on the streets they are re-working a murder. It is not unusual for family members to get an unexpected visit or phone call years after the crime, telling them there has finally been an arrest for the murder of their loved one.

After they review the file, the investigators set up an operational plan which often includes DNA testing, undercover operations, and wiretaps.

The changes in DNA evidence since 1990 have opened up incredible avenues for all Unsolved Homicide Units. "Ten years ago if you found plastic gloves at the scene, it meant the bad guy had some foresight," says Rolph. "Now it's to our benefit if they wear gloves because we aren't looking for fingerprints anymore. We're looking for DNA, and it's in the gloves."

And it takes just a speck of DNA to create a profile. It can come from cigarette butts, coffee cups, hair roots, clothing, and bite marks. Even water doesn't always wash away DNA.

* * *

In the Daniel Schraeder murder, DNA evidence would end up being at the forefront of the re-examination. Wayne Leatherdale and Larry Larin were the two officers from the Unsolved Homicide Unit assigned to the case. Sgt. Rolph helped in the early part of the examination.

A couple of problems had to be overcome first. The biggest was that the suspect, Billy Faulconer, had an airtight alibi for the time of Dan's death. It had been established by the original pathology report that from noon to 2 p.m. on January 18, 1991, he'd been at his mother's. The officers now wondered if that time period might be inaccurate.

Coroners usually determine the time of death by the rate at which a body cools. The officers wondered whether the amount of heat in the house from the fire had been taken into account when the time of death was determined. How long had the house been over-heated, and could the fire have artificially raised the temperature of the body, throwing the estimated time of death off? The coroner admitted he hadn't taken the fire into account. He re-evaluated the matter and came up with a new estimate, putting the time of death close to when the fire began.

This was an important step, except that it brought the officers to their next problem. The time of the fire had not actually been determined because it was already out when the fire fighters arrived.

The officers went back to the video taken by police at the original murder scene. They hoped it would help them pin down the time the fire had been set. What hadn't been noticed before was that on one of the walls of Dan's bungalow was an electric clock. In the RCMP forensics laboratory in February 1997, a forensics imaging technologist isolated two frames showing the clock, taken about 20 minutes apart. The time on the clock was the same in both frames, 6:12, suggesting that was when the power in the house went out as the fire spread. With this new information and the coroner's revised report, the time of Dan's death was put at 6:00 a.m. on January 18, 1991.

It would turn out to be a time for which Billy Faulconer had no alibi.

The unit still needed more to convict him, though, and they turned to the DNA evidence they knew was on the jeans. DNA, deoxyribonucleic acid, is a molecule present in every cell in every person's body. Everyone's DNA is unique (except identical twins, who share identical DNA). It's these differences that forensic scientists look at.

In the six years since the murder, DNA testing had become widely available. Aided by these advances, the police were able to match the blood on Billy's jeans to Dan. However, Billy lived on the streets and was known to be in the Schraeder house frequently, with or without Dan's invitation. He sometimes even slept there. According to Sgt. Rolph, the defence could say Dan accidentally cut his finger and got some blood on Billy's clothing when the younger man was with him. The police required one more piece of evidence. In the end, the dog would be the one to provide it.

In re-reading the report on the jeans, Weatherdale and Larin discovered mention of another foreign substance, likely canine blood. Animal DNA testing was scarce in 1997, and there was no expert in Canada capable of doing it. The officers turned to Dr. Joy Halverson and Zoogen Services Inc. in California for assistance. Dr. Halverson has been involved in animal DNA testing in criminal investigations for some time and has testified in a number of court cases. She founded Zoogen in 1989 as an independent laboratory for providing rapid and accurate DNA-based testing services related to different animal species.

The Schraeder case would become the first human murder Dr. Halverson would work on, but not the last. She and her colleague, Eric Johnston, worked with Dr. Gary Shutler of the RCMP forensic laboratory in Winnipeg, Manitoba.

Testing uses most of the same technologies for animal DNA as for humans, Halverson says. There are simply different sets of genetic markers for dogs, cats, and other animals. If you tried to test a dog sample using genetic markers for humans, there would simply be no result. In developing genetic markers for animals you go through much of the same process you would for humans.

The RCMP's Unsolved Homicide Unit was hopeful that Dr. Halverson would be able to help in their case against Billy Faulconer. After conducting the DNA testing, Dr. Halverson concluded that the chances of the blood on Billy's jeans coming from a dog other than Chico were one in 300 million.

"It was clearly the victim's dog's blood on the suspect," Sgt. Rolph says. "That's pretty much what put it over the top from there."

The mixture of Dan's and Chico's blood on his jeans was impossible for Billy to explain.

The officers went back over the crime scene for one

more look, specifically to study the blood splatter patterns to see if they would explain how and why the murder happened. There was a lot of blood on the walls and floor of the room. There was also blood in and around Dan's wheelchair, which indicated he was probably seated in it when the assault started. The officers even found blood on the fireplace. According to the blood splatter analyst, the dog had been held by the hind legs and its head smashed into the fireplace. Although the dog's body was found in the shed, this evidence conclusively placed Chico in the room when the murder occurred.

Finally, in September 1997, Billy Faulconer pleaded guilty to manslaughter and was sentenced to 10 years in prison. Daniel Schraeder and Chico's story would have one more moment in the spotlight. Their story was told in an episode of the Arts & Entertainment Network's *Cold Case Files*, watched by millions across North America.

Chapter 6
A Tragedy Within a Tragedy

he was a continent away from her homeland. So was he. When the lives of Janet Smith and Wong Foon Sing converged in 1924, it would leave one of them dead and the other being railroaded for her murder. The small fact of his innocence would not stop a group of eight men (including policemen) from kidnapping Wong and torturing him to try to obtain a confession.

What began on July 26, 1924, in Vancouver's wealthy Shaughnessy Heights would go on to become one of the most notorious and written-about unsolved murders in British Columbia's history. The events surrounding the death of a Scottish nursemaid would not only have ramifications for many of the city's elite, but would also highlight a deeply racist vein running through the province.

It was a hot Saturday morning and, at 3851 Osler Avenue (later renamed Osler Street), business as usual. Frederick L. Baker and his wife, Doreen, were waiting for their house on Nelson Street to be renovated. In the meantime, they were staying in the home of Frederick's brother, Richard P. Baker and his wife, Blanche, the oldest daughter of General Alexander McRae.

General McRae was among the richest men in Vancouver. He built and then lived in Hycroft mansion. By McRae's standards, the Bakers did not have great wealth — but their aunt, Lily Lefevre, did. On a social par with McRae, Mrs. Lefevre was the widow of Dr. John Lefevre, who had purchased land on the far side of False Creek just before the first bridge was built across it. She was left with a sizeable fortune which, through stock and other financial moves, she more than doubled after his death. With no children of her own, she took her sister's children — the Bakers — under her wing. They benefited well from her social standing in Vancouver, moving in privileged circles. Richard chose to work in the bank. Frederick articled with a law firm as a future lawyer.

Both Richard and Frederick had been pilots with

the Royal Flying Corps during World War I and both had survived being shot down (Richard by the "Red Baron," Baron Von Richthofen). Richard was captured and held as a prisoner of war, eventually returning to Vancouver a hero. This was certainly good enough for the General. After their marriage, Richard and Blanche McRae moved into the house on Osler Avenue.

Frederick recovered from his wounds in England. Soon after, on a trip back to Vancouver, he met Doreen Smith and they were married in 1922. The same year, they returned to London where, in November, their daughter Rosemary was born.

Doreen began to search for a nursemaid. In January 1923, she found the person she was looking for in Janet Smith, a 21-year-old woman who had been born in Perth, Scotland, but grown up in a working-class area of London. Janet was hired by the Bakers at the sum of $20 a month.

Before his marriage, Frederick had become a partner in a small London-based import-export business dealing in pharmaceuticals. There would be much speculation later on about his drug deals, legal and otherwise. In 1922, a ship arriving in Hong Kong was met by customs officers who arrested a Japanese citizen and seized four cases of furniture. Hidden in the furniture and the luggage of the prisoner were 60 kilograms of morphine and 70 kilograms of cocaine.

Documents found at the time led investigators to Howard Humphrey, a British businessman who worked for the import-export firm of Baker, Golwynne & Co. — the Baker being Frederick. As information from a Scotland Yard file would later reveal, Frederick had been in regular communication with some of the biggest drug dealers in Europe. He was part of a group that legally bought cocaine, heroin, morphine, and opium in Belgium and France and then shipped the drugs to Switzerland, after which they were smuggled to the Far East. In fact, Frederick was even more involved with illegal drug trafficking than Humphrey, but there had not been sufficient evidence to charge him. Nevertheless, shortly after Humphrey's conviction in the spring of 1923, Frederick moved his family to France briefly. Janet was delighted to go with them.

It was six months after that that the Bakers returned to Vancouver, again accompanied by Janet. They moved into a house on Nelson Street which they shared with Baker's mother.

In the spring of 1924, when Richard and Blanche Baker were leaving for an extended trip to Europe, they suggested that Frederick and his family move into their house on Osler Avenue. Richard had a Chinese "houseboy" named Wong Foon Sing who was to stay and work for Frederick's family while his boss was away. Wong had been in the employ of Richard for some time, and had his own room in the basement of the house.

Wong Foon Sing had come to Canada in 1913, leaving behind a wife and child in Hong Kong. Although a number of books and articles about the murder have said that Wong was 27 at the time, his immigration papers state clearly, "The above mentioned party who claims to be a native of Moy Wan in the District of Sun Wai of the age of 34 years arrived or landed at Vancouver on the 22nd day of June 1913." This would therefore have made Wong 45 years old when the murder of Janet Smith took place in 1924.

Once the family and Janet were settled in at Osler Avenue, the first couple of months passed without incident, including Smith's 22nd birthday. On Saturday, July 26, however, all that would change.

After taking Rosemary to the end of the short garden path to wave goodbye to her parents that morning, Janet went about her normal chores. She often sang while she worked and was later dubbed the "Scottish Nightingale" by the press. Workers building a house nearby would testify they heard her singing about 10:30 a.m. They stated they also saw Wong as he tended to the garden.

Some time after 11 a.m., Wong went to the kitchen

to clean the ice box. About the same time, he saw Janet take a load of laundry ready for ironing down the stairs from the kitchen into the basement. Wong was expecting the Bakers home for lunch and began to peel potatoes.

Suddenly he heard a loud bang.

"Did you know it was a revolver shot?" he was asked at a later inquest.

"I thought it was some gun. I didn't know," he replied.

Wong thought the noise came from outside and looked out the window. He saw nothing in the street and then went downstairs. Because it was a hot summer day, all the basement windows and the door leading outside were open. He found Janet lying on her back on the concrete floor. She was dressed in her blue denim dress with white stockings and shoes. Wong could see she was bleeding from her head. A .45 pistol lay about 15 centimetres from her hand and a flat iron lay between her right arm and her body. Not far from her right-hand side was a spent shell casing. Wong said he did not know what to do.

"I thought she was not dead," he recalled. He went to her and lifted up her head with both his hands. "I put her down and my hands were covered with blood." He wiped his hands on the lower part of his apron. When asked, Wong was adamant that he had not moved her body but merely raised and lowered her head. Janet's glasses were not on and Wong did not look for them. (The glasses were, in fact, broken and blood-stained and found later by the doctor at the scene.)

Wong said he did not run outside to look for help, but immediately ran upstairs and phoned Frederick at his office. He also called his uncle, Wong Ling Sai Jack, a long-time employee of well-known local lawyer Harry Senkler. Too frightened to return to the basement, Wong then went outside to wait for Frederick who was racing back to the house. He had misunderstood Wong's frantic talk about something happening to "nursie" and thought something had happened to his daughter in the nursery. After a quick trip up to the nursery, Frederick followed Wong to the basement. He put some water to Janet Smith's lips and felt for a pulse. There wasn't one. She was dead.

Frederick immediately phoned the Point Grey Police whose bungling, it would turn out (intentional or otherwise), ultimately created a murder mystery that could never be solved forensically.

(At about this time, amalgamation of the three separate police forces in the area — Point Grey, South Vancouver, and Vancouver — was being called for by many to improve the crime-solving abilities of officers in the region. Amalgamation eventually occurred in 1929, greatly helped along by the circumstances surrounding the Janet Smith case.)

The first officer on the scene was Constable James Green. He was in his 50s and had previously been a chief detective with the B.C. Provincial Police, a force whose reputation was only slightly better than that of the Point Grey Police. To this day, it is difficult to believe that he could have made so many mistakes in the case — but he did.

Constable Green arrived at the Baker house 10 to 15 minutes after Frederick's call and brought Dr. Bertie Blackwood with him. Green was led into the basement through the door from the garden. As Dr. Blackwood pronounced Janet dead, Green picked up the gun and handled it, as did Frederick, thereby obliterating any possibility of recovering fingerprints. Dr. Blackwood later testified that Janet's body was still warm when he arrived at the house and that she had been dead less than an hour.

Both the *Vancouver Sun* and *Vancouver Province* would report that during the first inquest, Frederick Baker stated the gun belonged to his brother, Richard. At the second inquest, however, he would testify that the .45 automatic army pistol belonged to him, a souvenir from his war days. It had been stored in his duffel bag in the hallway when they first moved in, he said, but after a couple of weeks he had asked Wong to move the bag to the attic. According to Frederick, the gun was loaded because he couldn't remove the jammed clip (magazine). He'd then simply put the safety catch on. Constable Green corroborated this and said he required Frederick's help at the scene to remove the clip.

Green looked over the death scene and then phoned his boss, Police Chief Hiram Simpson, telling him that in the 46 cases of suicide he had seen in his career, this was the clearest.

Undertaker John Edwards then received a call from a Point Grey Police officer (likely Chief Simpson) who told him to go ahead and embalm the body. Edwards was uncomfortable with this because it had been a violent death and the autopsy had not yet been done. He phoned Coroner Brydone-Jack, who instructed the undertaker and his assistants to go ahead and embalm and pack the body and have it ready for the inquest. As they undressed Janet's body, they threw the clothes into a pile on the floor. The blood seeped through all the clothes, muddying any helpful evidence even further. They did note two strange burns on Janet's right side.

The case was now wrapping up quickly for the police, but within a day rumours had already started to grow. An inquest was set for Tuesday, July 29. On the Monday, Constable Green decided to visit the crime scene again. Lo and behold, this time he found the bullet which had escaped his notice on the day Janet died. Experiments done months later would show that a bullet going through a skull would have marks on it. This bullet had none — but then the pistol found near the body would never actually be proven to be the murder weapon either.

At the first inquest, a number of people would testify that Janet was a cheerful girl who would never kill herself. Frederick would put forth the theory that Janet had been curious about the gun and was examining it when it went off. Why, in the middle of ironing, she would go up to the attic and get the gun and take it back to the basement before examining it he couldn't say.

Some disturbing evidence was given in regard to the post-embalming autopsy, done by Dr. Archibald Hunter. He testified there were no powder burns on the surface or under the skin of Janet Smith as there would have been if she had held the gun near to herself and pulled the trigger. Both he and a Dr. Mullen told the jury that a gunshot wound alone would not cause the damage found inside the girl's skull, although they could not determine how that damage was inflicted. They speculated that it could have been caused by a sharp blow to the side of the head.

The lack of evidence aside, the jury was quick to

enter a verdict. Janet Smith, they said, had accidentally shot herself.

As far as Chief Simpson was concerned, this was the end of the Janet Smith affair. He stated there was no evidence given to suggest foul play and there was nothing more to be done by the Point Grey Police regarding the jury's verdict.

That may have been true, but there was much more to be done by many other organizations and individuals.

Members of the United Council of Scottish Societies were very vocal from the beginning that Smith had been murdered, and they were not about to let the case go. In the 1920s, Scots made up one-third of Vancouver's population of 250,000 and had tremendous power. Many of their members had an intense hatred of "Orientals " and, in this case, had convinced themselves that Wong Foon Sing was the killer. They would stop at nothing to bring about his conviction. And other nursemaids in Vancouver also believed their friend had been murdered. Mary ("Cissy") Jones in particular was adamant that Janet would not have taken her own life, and was equally as adamant that Wong had. She went to the one place where she knew she would get a hearing.

Someone who hated the Chinese more than Cissy was Reverend Duncan McDougall. From his pulpit, and anywhere he had an audience, he would rail against the Chinese. He even started publishing a monthly journal in 1924 which ran for two years and regularly featured articles about the Janet Smith murder and the "yellow peril." His journal was called *The Beacon* and its purported intent was "shedding light on dark places" — which it certainly did, although probably not in the way the Reverend intended. In addition to the Chinese, he attacked the Japanese, Jews, and Catholics. One issue even contained an article in strong support of the Ku Klux Klan in Canada.

Cissy Jones had a receptive ear in McDougall and he helped keep the rumours and agitation going against Wong Foon Sing.

The United Council of Scottish Societies hired lawyer Alex Henderson as their legal advisor and chief investigator. However, the Chinese also had strong support systems. They met at the Oriental Club where many "tong" functions were held. (Tongs were a cross between a Chinese guild or association and a secret society.) One of the largest tongs at that time in British Columbia, the Lim Tong, hired Harry Senkler to defend Wong in future proceedings. It would turn out to be a full-time job in the racist climate of Vancouver.

The prejudice against Asians was evident all across Canada at that time. A head tax of $50 was imposed on all Chinese immigrants in 1885 and was raised to $100 in 1901 and finally to $500 in 1905. In 1907, race riots swept through Vancouver's Chinatown. People of Chinese descent could not become Canadian citizens, and therefore could not vote or become lawyers or doctors. Many Chinese men came to Canada in the hopes of making a better life, with the intent of bringing their wives and children over later. However, the Canadian government made sure that wouldn't happen when they passed the Chinese Immigration Act in 1923, barring any further Chinese immigration.

Following the hasty first inquest, the persistent efforts of the Scottish Societies paid off. By the beginning of August, it was announced that Inspector Forbes Cruickshank of the B.C. Provincial Police would take over the case. The Scots were happy with this development and felt sure the arrest of Wong was just around the corner. They were not far off.

Police often hired detectives outside the police force to "help" them with their investigations. This often led to suspects being roughed up. Cruickshank turned to the Canadian Detective Agency for such a man, Oscar Robinson. It was reported in the paper on August 13, 1924, that Wong had been picked up at Carrall and Cordova Streets by the Provincial Police the night before and taken to police headquarters for questioning. The truth was a little different. Wong was taken by Oscar Robinson to his detective bureau's offices on Hastings Street. Among those present, Wong later identified Inspector Cruickshank. Wong was subjected to seven hours of grilling, but stuck to his story before being released at 3 a.m.

Alexander Malcom Manson was a lawyer and Liberal politician. He was also Attorney General of British Columbia from 1922 to 1924. His role in the subsequent investigation and brutal mistreatment of Wong was never completely exposed, but he was described in one of the papers as having an intense hatred of Orientals. He was hearing the rumours and could see that the notion of "cover-up" was growing and beginning to gather steam. Something had to be done. The day after Wong's "questioning," Manson's office officially stated that Janet Smith did not come to her death by either suicide or accident. This left only murder.

On August 25, 1924, Manson authorized an application to a Supreme Court judge for exhumation of the body of Janet Smith. The second autopsy would be done by Dr. G.F. Curtis and a date for the inquest set shortly. At the same time, Manson announced a new public inquiry would be held into the mystery of Smith's death. Although he claimed no pressure had been put on him to do this, it was well known that he was pressured from numerous camps. He appointed Charles Craig as counsel for the Department of the Attorney General.

The autopsy was performed by five doctors on August 28 and Janet's body was then held in the morgue until the second inquest, which began on September 4 amid a scene never witnessed before in Vancouver. The rampant speculation over her death and suspicions of a cover-up had created great interest throughout the city. Everyone wanted to be at the inquest, but the court only held 50. The crowds swelled to 500 people and became rowdy. Many young domestics had come to hear what had happened to one of their own and they brought lunches with them in order not to miss a thing.

The inquest was closed to the general public until 10:20 a.m. The lawyers, police, and newspaper reporters were the only ones allowed inside with the judge and jury, and this incited the crowd even more. They began to bang on the doors and demand entry.

"What have you to hide in there?" someone shouted. "Open the door. Let us in!"

Finally the doors opened and the 50 seats were filled. James Wilson, a former Liverpool policeman, was chosen foreman of the jury. The banging and shouting of those left in the hallway continued throughout the day. Those in attendance were disappointed because at 10:27 a.m. the session was suspended so that the jury could go to the morgue to view the body and then to the Baker house on Osler Avenue to view the crime scene.

The only evidence the jury saw of Janet's violent death as they viewed her remains at the morgue was the hole in her right temple above her eye. Dr. Hunter, who had done the first autopsy, pointed out that a wire had been run through the wound to show the direction of the bullet. It entered near and slightly above the right eyebrow. And Dr. Curtis, who had done the second autopsy, said the angle of entry indicated Janet's head had been level with the gun when the shot was fired. Dr. Hunter also brought to the jury's attention a black smudge on a finger of her left hand, and he showed them the two burn marks made by the iron on her right side. Despite numerous attempts by various expert witnesses, it was never satisfactorily explained how Janet could have fallen and grabbed the iron in such a way as to leave the two burns marks on her side.

After leaving the morgue, the group went to the Baker house. In an ironic twist, Wong, who had no idea they would be coming, was in the basement ironing when they all arrived.

Dr. Blackwood then explained what he saw on his arrival that July day. He said Janet's head lay partly on a block of wood. The wood was still there and the doctor placed it into the correct position. He said she lay across the passage to the laundry tubs, with her head under one corner of a tub and her feet under the ironing table. Her clothes were bunched up a little under her, Dr. Blackwood said. The flat iron, which had been torn loose from its socket, was between her right arm and her body and had burned both that arm and her torso.

Dr. Brydone-Jack then told Wong to lie down on the basement floor in the position of the body. Wong was reluctant to do so, partly because he had a clean shirt and collar on, but finally he conceded. They then placed the iron and the gun in their respective positions. At this point, most of the focus was on two indentations in the basement floor and one in the wall and whether or not these had been caused by bullets. The question was raised once again about the possibility that Janet had been killed by a blow to the head and then shot to make the murder look like suicide or an accident. In coming weeks, these marks would be speculated on endlessly, but no conclusion was reached at that time.

The trial proceedings then returned to the courtroom. Wong Foon Sing was to be called next, but that had to be postponed for a day so that preparations could be made for the chicken oath (see Chapter 2).

Constable Green had earlier denied he made a comment to Point Grey Police Chief Simpson regarding the certainty of suicide. When Simpson took the stand, however, he stated the officer had told him it was the clearest case of suicide he had ever seen.

In explaining why he had not found the bullet on the day of the murder, Green also claimed he had not done a thorough search of the murder scene. Dr. Blackwood testified that he in fact saw Green do a very thorough search, especially of the floor.

Dr. Curtis testified he believed it highly unlikely that Janet had committed suicide. In addition to there being no powder burns on the body, he said that she should have crumpled to the floor after the shot, rather than lying out straight on her back. He also reported that, although the embalming had ruined her internal organs, medical evidence showed the young woman had died a virgin.

The major piece of evidence to be looked at in the second inquest was the content of Janet's diaries. While a number of witnesses testified that she had lived in fear of the Chinese man, her diaries showed no such fear.

"Sing is awfully devoted," she wrote just three days before her death. "He gave me two rolls of film for my camera, also sweets, and does all my [personal] washing and ironing."

A friend of Janet's also admitted that two days before her death, Janet and Wong had snapped some shots of each other with her camera. Still the friend insisted Janet had been afraid of him.

Janet's diaries also revealed she had many boyfriends in addition to her fiancé. Most of the entries revolved around men, reflecting Janet's own admission that she was a bit of a flirt.

As he did at the first inquest, Frederick Baker testified he had trouble getting the magazine out of the gun and so had left it loaded. At the request of the Attorney General's counsel, Charles Craig, Inspector Forbes Cruickshank of the Provincial Police demonstrated that the magazine could be extracted from the gun — the supposed murder weapon — with ease.

Finally, it was Wong's turn on the stand. He simply repeated the same story he had been telling from the beginning.

The inquest's verdict was a foregone conclusion: "We find that Janet K. Smith was, on July 26, wilfully murdered in the course of her employment in the laundry of the basement of F.L. Baker's home by being shot through the head, but by whom we do not know."

For all the mistakes he made early on in the investigation, Constable Green was simply given a slap on the wrist. Interestingly, although he had earned only about $1,200 a year as a Point Grey policeman, he managed to buy half-ownership in a Vancouver hotel after he left the force in 1926.

Attorney General Manson was feeling the heat of criticism for the murder mystery that wouldn't die. He appointed Malcom Bruce Jackson to undertake an investigation of the case. Jackson, a defeated Member of the Legislative Assembly (MLA) and close friend of Manson, came on board in the fall of 1924. The United Council of Scottish Societies was delighted, feeling that interest in the Janet Smith murder would again take centre stage. The police, however, were unhappy as Jackson began to dig around. In spite of all his pronouncements that vital information was surfacing and he was getting to the bottom of the murder, in truth Jackson was not any further ahead than anyone else at that point.

Mary Ellen Smith (no relation to Janet) was the Liberal MLA for Vancouver and the first woman ever elected to the B.C. Legislative Assembly. On November 5, 1924, a group of women from the Scottish Societies met with Smith in Victoria. They were, they said, concerned that Chinese servants were corrupting the moral standards of white girls. Mrs. Smith agreed with them and introduced the "Janet Smith bill" in the legislature. The bill would have made it illegal for anyone to employ Chinese domestics and white women in the same household. The ensuing comments from numerous quarters were among the most prejudiced ever heard in the legislature.

Smith's private member's bill died on the floor December 12, 1924, but not because most critics of the bill objected to it from an outraged sense of morality. Rather, most of them were concerned the bill would cause employers to get rid of white workers in favour of the generally more efficient, less well-paid Chinese workers.

There is no argument that the murder of Janet Smith was a tragedy, but what happened next was equally tragic.

On March 20, 1925, Richard and Blanche Baker, who had moved back into their home a week after Janet's murder, went out for the evening. Wong had finished eating his dinner around 7:35 p.m. He left the basement window open while he was in his room changing his clothes.

"I washed my face and got ready to go out," he later said. He locked the door behind him as he left and thought he heard a dog barking in the garage. He started to walk towards the street, but something didn't feel right to him.

"Sometimes robbers in Shaughnessy Heights," he testified.

He went back and unlocked the basement door. Looking in, he called, "Is anyone there?" No answer.

Suddenly, before he knew what was happening, three men attacked him. One of them struck his head with a flashlight. They were all in white robes and hoods with eye holes.

"They used force on my neck and then threw me on the cement steps," Wong was later quoted as saying. "They gagged me and put a cloth over my eyes. They locked my hands with handcuffs and also my feet. …One man said to the others, 'Give me a gun and I'll kill the bastard.'"

Before they carried Wong off, they broke the locked door to his bedroom and turned everything upside down, taking some of his belongings with them. They then drove him around for hours, even going through a ruse to make him think they had crossed the border into the United States. In the end, they only took him a short distance away, to 3543 West 25th (later named King Edward Avenue).

For the next 42 days, Wong Foon Sing's life was a nightmare of torture and brutality that would leave him with broken ribs, a burst eardrum, and a fractured skull. As a result of all the beatings, he would be left with constant buzzing in his head and deafness in one ear. Two weeks after they kidnapped him, Wong's abductors even attempted to hang him — and they almost succeeded. After that, the physical cruelty eased a little, but not the mental torment. He was shackled to a bed with chains that were secured through holes in the floor. And guns were always present.

"When they let me up to wash or go to the bathroom, there was always a man with me carrying a gun," Wong testified.

Meanwhile, when Richard Baker awoke the morning after the abduction, he knew instantly that something was wrong because the house was cold. Wong always had the house heated by the time he arose. On finding his houseboy missing, Richard immediately phoned the Vancouver Police, not wanting to deal with the Point Grey force. Before long, rumours of an abduction were circulating, as well as rumours that the authorities were behind it.

On May 1, Wong's kidnappers blindfolded him and drove him around for a couple of hours before finally releasing him at 3:00 a.m. on Marine Drive. Within a minute, he was found wandering in a daze by the Point Grey Police. All he wanted to do was return to Osler Avenue, but instead the police took him to the station and booked him for the murder of Janet Smith.

Sadly, outraged reaction to the abhorrent treatment of Wong was restricted to the Chinese community and a few newspaper editorial writers.

"If any Englishman or Canadian had been treated

in this manner in any foreign country, it would have been cause for war," a *Vancouver Sun* editorial stated in May 1925. "Why should British justice set a higher standard for a Britisher in China than for a Chinaman in Canada?"

"If Wong Foon Sing is guilty of this murder, hang him," the editorial continued. "But that is something for the courts to decide. It has nothing to do with the methods tried to get him to talk. Even if Wong should be guiltier than sin, to condone or gloss over this outrageous banditry is simply to wipe out all the years between 1215 and 1925. ...This is Canada, where such things MUST not happen."

Reverend McDougall, still intent on shedding light in dark places in *The Beacon*, was not happy. "Whether it was the same priest who heard the confessions of the Baker family," McDougall wrote in his monthly journal," who also directed the conscience of the editor of the *Sun*, or whether it was a natural yellow streak in himself that made him more concerned about the feelings of a yellow man than about the life of a white girl, we cannot tell."

He also said the editor should be charged with contempt.

Wong was being kept incommunicado in Oakalla Prison. When his lawyer, Harry Senkler, found out, he

The front page of the *Evening Sun* dated Friday May 1, 1925
featuring the story of Wong's arrest for murder

was furious and threatened legal action. He was quickly allowed to see his client. The Chinese Consul called for a royal commission into Wong's kidnapping and Attorney General Manson scrambled to distance himself from a kidnapping he most likely knew about.

When Senkler finally managed to see Wong, he was very concerned about the man's physical condition and asked permission for doctors to see him. Dr. P. McLennan reported that Wong's injuries were much more severe than he expected and he brought in other doctors. With a fractured skull and broken ribs, a black eye and deafened ear, Wong looked in bad shape when reporters saw him on his way to have more X-rays.

The preliminary hearing for Wong on the murder charge began May 8, 1925. Even Manson, who had acknowledged to several authorities (including the police) that he didn't think Wong was the killer, said he hoped charging Wong would "smoke out the real killer."

The preliminary hearing revealed little new evidence except for the results of ballistics tests and the manner in which they were conducted. Inspector Cruickshank said the tests were done with a gun similar to the presumed murder weapon. The head severed from a pig had first been used to conduct some of the ballistics experiments. The gun was fired three times, 20 centimetres from the target. In each case, the spent bullets were misshapen, unlike the pristine one found by Green at the crime scene. There were also powder burns on the pig's head each time. A gasp came from the crowd at Cruickshank's next statement. He said that a decapitated human head had been used in the final experiment — the head of a dead mental patient at Essondale Hospital in New Westminster who had had no family or friends to claim his body. The ballistics test on the head also produced damaged bullets.

Later that year, Manson was forced to defend this "corpse riddling" in the legislature.

There was clearly still no direct evidence linking Wong to Janet's murder. Nevertheless, he was committed for trial.

Senkler, who had been working furiously all this time, was finally able to get Wong released on bail on June 24, 1925.

At last, however, the law was beginning to gain on the kidnappers. Officials had found the house where Wong had been held and he was taken there to verify it. On June 17, three men were arrested for the kidnapping of Wong — Oscar Robinson of the Canadian Detective Bureau, his son William, and Varity Norton, employed by the Detective Bureau. Summonses were also issued for eight others, four of them officers with the Point Grey Police. On July 9, 1925, the Crown dropped some of

Janet Smith's tombstone

the charges, but committed eight of the men for trial, including three of the Point Grey officers.

They were tried in November 1925. Oscar Robinson was sentenced to a year in jail, Norton received nine months, and one of the remaining defendants was fined $200. None of the others was convicted.

In September 1925, the unveiling of Janet Smith's tombstone in Mountain View Cemetery brought a crowd of more than 4,000 people. Paid for by the Scottish Societies and donations, the single pillar has a broken top, the Scottish symbol for an early death. The stone reads in part, "On Earth, one gentle soul the less; in Heaven, one angel more."

On October 9, 1925, after less than two days of deliberation, a grand jury found there was no evidence to send Wong to trial for murder. His nightmare was finally over. He went back to work at Richard Baker's house, but in March 1926 decided that, after almost 13 years in Canada, it was time to return to China. Senkler informed the authorities of his client's intentions and no one stopped Wong from leaving.

Janet Smith's murder started off as the sad death of a nursemaid, but went on to represent much more than that. The fact her killer has never been found has only added to the allure of this mystery. A play and numerous books have been written about it and Janet's ghost is even said to inhabit Hycroft mansion. Events connected with the murder were talked about in British Columbia and in Ottawa for years. *The Canadian Annual Review (of Public Affairs)* contained a short summation of the case in its 1925 volume. As was noted there, Attorney General Manson was criticized in the British Columbia legislature by the opposition for the way the investigation had been conducted.

He vigorously defended himself, saying, "I have tried to maintain the administration of justice untarnished in this Province. I would with all my heart that these pages in our history had not been written."

Both Janet Smith and Wong Foon Sing would, no doubt, agree.

Bibliography

Greenwood, F. Murray and Beverley Boissery. *Uncertain Justice: Canadian Women and Capital Punishment, 1754-1953*. Toronto, ON: Dundurn Press, 2000.

Okeefe, Betty and Ian Macdonald. *Canadian Holy War: A Story of Clans, Tongs, Murder, and Bigotry*. Surrey, BC: Heritage House, 2000.

Robin, Martin. *The Saga of Red Ryan and Other Tales of Violence from Canada's Past*. Saskatoon, SK: Western Producer Prairie Books, 1982.

Starkins, Edward. *Who Killed Janet Smith?* Toronto, ON: Macmillan of Canada, 1984.

Taylor, Martin R. *The Investigation of the Murder of Molly Justice*. Victoria, BC: Ministry of Attorney General, 1996.

Acknowledgments

I want to thank all the writers who came before me, leaving a trail of history to follow in news clippings, magazine articles, and books. I am grateful to all of you.

Thanks so much to my friend Seema Shah, who patiently listened to my endless tales of murder and intrigue. She read each chapter and helped me iron out any kinks, making the process of writing this book so much easier.

I owe a debt of gratitude to a number of departments in the Vancouver Public Library — Social Sciences, Special Collections, and especially the newspaper division. They all gave me much-needed assistance. Thanks also to the staffs of the Vancouver Public Archives and the National Public Archives in Ottawa.

To Sgt. Trent Rolph of the RCMP, who gave me invaluable insights into his seven years of work with British Columbia's Unsolved Homicide Unit, I thank you.

I also wish to thank my editor, Georgina Montgomery, for all her efforts to make this a better book than it would have been without her.

And, finally, many thanks to all the cats in my life who have supported both myself and my writing — you know who you are.

About the Author

Susan McNicoll lives in Port Coquitlam, BC, where she divides her time between writing and running her own bookkeeping business. Although she is now a die-hard British Columbian, her heart still belongs to the Toronto Blue Jays. Susan's lifelong love of words and history has been the main focus of her writing career, which began with five years as a reporter for the Ottawa Journal. With this *Amazing Stories* title she has been able to indulge her interests in the use of forensic science and the criminal mind.

Susan spent 11 years writing a book on post-war Canadian theatre history, which is scheduled to be published in 2004.

Photo Credits

Cover: BC Archives; **BC Archives:** pages 38 and 127; **Susan McNicoll:** page 130.

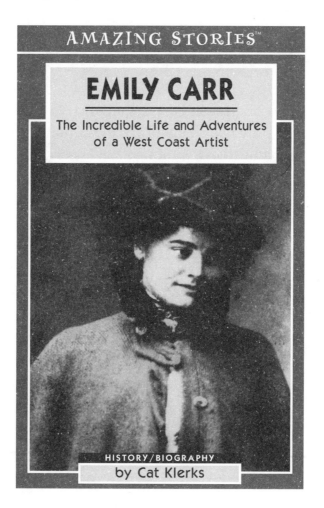

Emily Carr
ISBN 1-55153-996-9

NOW AVAILABLE!

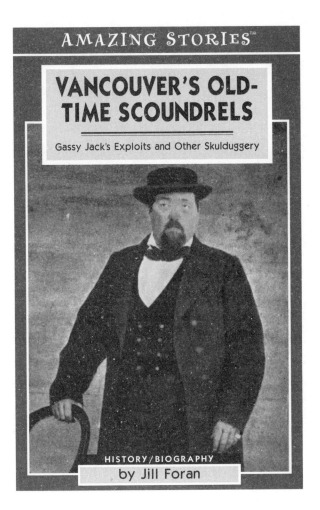

AMAZING STORIES™

VANCOUVER'S OLD-TIME SCOUNDRELS

Gassy Jack's Exploits and Other Skulduggery

HISTORY/BIOGRAPHY
by Jill Foran

Vancouver's Old-Time Scoundrels
ISBN 1-55153-989-6

AMAZING STORIES™

RATTENBURY

The Life and Tragic End
of BC's Greatest Architect

HISTORY/BIOGRAPHY
by Stan Sauerwein

Rattenbury
ISBN 1-55153-981-0

OTHER AMAZING STORIES

These titles are available wherever you buy books. If you have trouble finding the book you want, call the Altitude order desk at 1-800-957-6888, e-mail your request to: orderdesk@altitudepublishing.com or visit our Web site at www.amazingstories.ca

All titles retail for $9.95 Cdn or $7.95 US. (Prices subject to change.)

New AMAZING STORIES titles are published every month. If you would like more information, e-mail your name and mailing address to: amazingstories@altitudepublishing.com.

NOW AVAILABLE!

AMAZING STORIES™

TALES FROM THE WEST COAST

Smugglers, Sea Monsters, and Other Stories

HISTORY/ADVENTURE
by Adrienne Mason

Tales from the West Coast
ISBN 1-55153-986-1